EMERGING CYBER THREATS TO THE UNITED STATES

HEARING

BEFORE THE

SUBCOMMITTEE ON CYBERSECURITY, INFRASTRUCTURE PROTECTION, AND SECURITY TECHNOLOGIES

OF THE

COMMITTEE ON HOMELAND SECURITY HOUSE OF REPRESENTATIVES

ONE HUNDRED FOURTEENTH CONGRESS

SECOND SESSION

FEBRUARY 25, 2016

Serial No. 114–55

Printed for the use of the Committee on Homeland Security

Available via the World Wide Web: http://www.gpo.gov/fdsys/

U.S. GOVERNMENT PUBLISHING OFFICE

21–527 PDF   WASHINGTON : 2016

For sale by the Superintendent of Documents, U.S. Government Publishing Office
Internet: bookstore.gpo.gov   Phone: toll free (866) 512–1800; DC area (202) 512–1800
Fax: (202) 512–2104   Mail: Stop IDCC, Washington, DC 20402–0001

COMMITTEE ON HOMELAND SECURITY

MICHAEL T. McCAUL, Texas, *Chairman*

LAMAR SMITH, Texas
PETER T. KING, New York
MIKE ROGERS, Alabama
CANDICE S. MILLER, Michigan, *Vice Chair*
JEFF DUNCAN, South Carolina
TOM MARINO, Pennsylvania
LOU BARLETTA, Pennsylvania
SCOTT PERRY, Pennsylvania
CURT CLAWSON, Florida
JOHN KATKO, New York
WILL HURD, Texas
EARL L. "BUDDY" CARTER, Georgia
MARK WALKER, North Carolina
BARRY LOUDERMILK, Georgia
MARTHA McSALLY, Arizona
JOHN RATCLIFFE, Texas
DANIEL M. DONOVAN, JR., New York

BENNIE G. THOMPSON, Mississippi
LORETTA SANCHEZ, California
SHEILA JACKSON LEE, Texas
JAMES R. LANGEVIN, Rhode Island
BRIAN HIGGINS, New York
CEDRIC L. RICHMOND, Louisiana
WILLIAM R. KEATING, Massachusetts
DONALD M. PAYNE, JR., New Jersey
FILEMON VELA, Texas
BONNIE WATSON COLEMAN, New Jersey
KATHLEEN M. RICE, New York
NORMA J. TORRES, California

BRENDAN P. SHIELDS, *Staff Director*
JOAN V. O'HARA, *General Counsel*
MICHAEL S. TWINCHEK, *Chief Clerk*
I. LANIER AVANT, *Minority Staff Director*

———

SUBCOMMITTEE ON CYBERSECURITY, INFRASTRUCTURE PROTECTION, AND SECURITY TECHNOLOGIES

JOHN RATCLIFFE, Texas, *Chairman*

PETER T. KING, New York
TOM MARINO, Pennsylvania
SCOTT PERRY, Pennsylvania
CURT CLAWSON, Florida
DANIEL M. DONOVAN, JR., New York
MICHAEL T. McCAUL, Texas *(ex officio)*

CEDRIC L. RICHMOND, Louisiana
LORETTA SANCHEZ, California
SHEILA JACKSON LEE, Texas
JAMES R. LANGEVIN, Rhode Island
BENNIE G. THOMPSON, Mississippi *(ex officio)*

BRETT DeWITT, *Subcommittee Staff Director*
JOHN DICKHAUS, *Subcommittee Clerk*
CHRISTOPHER SCHEPIS, *Minority Subcommittee Staff Director*

CONTENTS

EMERGING CYBER THREATS TO THE UNITED STATES

Thursday, February 25, 2016

U.S. HOUSE OF REPRESENTATIVES,
COMMITTEE ON HOMELAND SECURITY,
SUBCOMMITTEE ON CYBERSECURITY, INFRASTRUCTURE
PROTECTION, AND SECURITY TECHNOLOGIES,
Washington, DC.

The subcommittee met, pursuant to call, at 2:06 p.m., in Room 311, Cannon House Office Building, Hon. John Ratcliffe [Chairman of the subcommittee] presiding.

Present: Representatives Ratcliffe, McCaul, Marino, Donovan, Richmond, and Jackson Lee.

Mr. RATCLIFFE. Good afternoon. The Committee on Homeland Security Subcommittee on Cybersecurity, Infrastructure Protection, and Security Technologies will come to order.

The subcommittee is meeting today to examine the evolving cybersecurity threats from nation-states such as China, Russia, North Korea, and Iran, as well as cyber threats from criminal organizations and terrorist groups such as ISIS.

Over the last several years, we have seen these actors continue to develop and build even more sophisticated cyber capabilities. In 2016, these hackers pose an even greater threat to the U.S. homeland and our critical infrastructure. To put it simply, cybersecurity is National security.

In 2015, the Nation was victim to one of the most significant cyber attacks in our history. The breach at the Office of Personnel Management exposed the personal and extremely sensitive security clearance information of 21.5 million current and former Government employees. In 2014, we saw North Korea conduct a cyber attack on Sony Pictures that not only destroyed computers, but also sought to muzzle free speech and threaten American ideals.

Unfortunately, the administration's lack of proportional responses to these cyber attacks has demonstrated to the world that there are no real consequences for such actions. Without a comprehensive National cybersecurity strategy that addresses deterrence effectively, I worry that 2016 could bring an increasing number of those willing to push the boundaries.

In recent news, a lot of attention was directed at the Hollywood Presbyterian Medical Center in Los Angeles that was a victim of a ransomware attack. This type of malware infects victims' computers and locks them until a payment, or a "ransom," is made. The medical center was forced to pay $17,000 to restore its systems.

But this isn't a problem unique to Hollywood. In my own district in Northeast Texas, the Titus Regional Medical Center suffered a similar attack. Their electronic health record system was locked, and they weren't able to access patient information.

Of the nation states, Russia continues to rank near the top in terms of capabilities, with increasing aggression across the globe that may continue to manifest itself in cyber space. The director of national intelligence, James Clapper, told the Senate Armed Services Committee in September that the Russian government is establishing its own central cyber command that will be responsible for carrying out offensive cyber operations.

China also ranks high in terms of capability, and it continues to pose a significant threat to the United States in terms of cyber espionage and the theft of intellectual property. In September, the administration announced an agreement with the Chinese government to refrain from engaging in hacking of our intellectual property. I look forward to hearing today from our industry witnesses on their thoughts about the success of this agreement.

Iran continues to emerge as a top cybersecurity threat, as well. While many would argue that its intent to carry out its attacks is strong, it still lags behind other nation-states in terms of capabilities. However, the administration's recent nuclear agreement with Iran could have unintended consequences in cyber space, as the lifting of economic sanctions could provide the influx of cash to fuel the development of cybersecurity capabilities.

Criminal organizations continue to pose a great risk to the American people, as we have seen with breaches at places like Target and Home Depot, which exposed the credit card information of millions of people. While the intent of criminal groups may be different from nation-states, the impact on everyday Americans is felt very directly.

Last, terrorist groups such as ISIS may currently lack the capability to pose a major cybersecurity threat to the United States. But given the vast resources this group has amassed, developing or purchasing sophisticated cyber tools is not far out of reach. ISIS followers and the so-called Cyber Caliphate have had success in hacking social media accounts of our military personnel and posting home addresses and other personal information on-line, asking followers to carry out attacks.

In late 2015, Congress, recognizing these threats, enacted the Cybersecurity Act of 2015. The act establishes the Department of Homeland Security National Cybersecurity and Communications Integration Center, or NCCIC, as the sole civilian interface for sharing cyber threat information with the Federal Government. The act establishes liability protections for companies to share information with DHS and among themselves.

In light of this legislation, we hope that the private sector will share more with each other and with the Government, and we look forward to hearing from our witnesses today on what they are doing to increase information sharing.

In response to the devastating attack on OPM, the act bolsters DHS's ability to deploy intrusion detection and prevention capabilities across our Federal Government. These capabilities will ensure the proper capabilities to defend Government networks from nation-state attacks.

Unfortunately, cyber threat actors—be they nation states, criminal groups, or terrorist organizations—remain undeterred, continuing to conduct cyber attacks. The problem is compounded by the lack of acceptable norms in cyber space, and I have questions on whether or not the administration's lack of response to these attacks has deterred or even emboldened our adversaries.

The President recently announced a Cybersecurity National Action Plan. Whether this is too little too late, and the clarity of the overall guidance behind the plan, remains to be seen as we watch the most meaningful part of any grand plan—its execution. In this day and age, there is agreement that the battle for security of our information systems is continually escalating. The testimony today will help inform what actions Congress can take to further the interests of our National security.

[The statement of Mr. Ratcliffe follows:]

STATEMENT OF CHAIRMAN JOHN RATCLIFFE

FEBRUARY 25, 2016

The subcommittee is meeting today to examine the evolving cybersecurity threats from nation-states such as China, Russia, North Korea, and Iran, as well as cyber threats from criminal organizations and terrorist groups such as ISIS. Over the last several years we have seen these actors continue to develop and build even more sophisticated cyber capabilities. In 2016, these hackers pose an even greater threat to the U.S. homeland and our critical infrastructure. To put it simply, cybersecurity is National security.

In 2015, the Nation was victim to one of the most significant cyber attacks in history. The breach at the Office of Personnel Management exposed the personal and extremely sensitive security clearance information of 21.5 million current and former Government employees. In 2014, we saw North Korea conduct a cyber attack on Sony Pictures that not only destroyed computers, but also sought to muzzle free speech and threaten American ideals.

Unfortunately, the administration's lack of proportional responses to these cyber attacks has demonstrated to the world that there are no real consequences for such actions. Without a comprehensive National cybersecurity strategy that addresses deterrence effectively, I worry that 2016 could bring an increasing number of those willing to push the boundaries.

In recent news, a lot of attention was directed at the Hollywood Presbyterian Medical Center in Los Angeles that was a victim of a ransomware attack. This type of malware infects victims' computers and locks them until a payment, or a "ransom," is made. The medical center was forced to pay $17,000 to restore its systems. But this isn't unique to Hollywood. In my own district in Northeast Texas, the Titus Regional Medical Center suffered a similar attack. Their electronic health record system was locked and they weren't able to access patient information.

Of the nation-state threats, Russia continues to rank near the top in terms of capabilities, with increasing aggression across the globe that may continue to manifest itself in cyber space. The Director of National Intelligence, James Clapper, told the Senate Armed Services Committee in September that the Russian government is establishing its own central cyber command that will be responsible for carrying out offensive cyber operations.

China also ranks high in terms of capability and continues to pose a significant threat to the United States in terms of cyber espionage and theft of intellectual property. In September, the administration announced an agreement with the Chinese government to refrain from engaging in hacking of intellectual property. I look forward to hearing today from our industry witnesses today on their thoughts about the success of this agreement.

Iran continues to emerge as a top cybersecurity threat. While many would argue that its intent to carry out attacks is strong, it still lags behind other nation-states in capabilities. However, the administration's recent nuclear agreement with Iran could have unintended consequences in cyber space, as the lifting of economic sanctions could provide influx of cash to fuel the development of cybersecurity capabilities.

Criminal organizations continue to pose a great risk to the American people, as we have seen with the breaches of Target and Home Depot, which exposed the credit card information of millions of people. While the intent of criminal groups may be different from nation-states, the impact on everyday Americans is felt very directly.

Lastly, terrorist groups such as ISIS may currently lack the capability to pose a major cybersecurity threat to United States. But given the vast resources the group has amassed, developing or purchasing sophisticated cyber tools is not far out of reach. ISIS followers and the so-called Cyber Caliphate have had success in hacking social media accounts of military personnel and posting home addresses and other personal information on-line asking followers to carry out attacks.

In late 2015, Congress—recognizing these threats—enacted the Cybersecurity Act of 2015. The Act establishes the Department of Homeland Security, National Cybersecurity and Communications Integration Center (NCCIC) as the sole civilian interface for sharing of cyber threat information with the Federal Government. The Act establishes liability protections for companies to share information with DHS, and among themselves. In light of this legislation, we hope the private sector will share more with each other and the Government, and we look forward to hearing from our witnesses on what they are doing to increase information sharing.

In response to the devastating attack on OPM, the Act bolsters DHS's ability to deploy intrusion detection and prevention capabilities across the Federal Government. These capabilities will ensure the proper capabilities to defend Government networks from these nation-state attacks.

Unfortunately, cyber threat actors—be they nation states, criminal groups, or terrorist organizations—remain undeterred, continuing to conduct cyber attacks. This problem is compounded by the lack of acceptable norms in cyber space and I have questions on whether or not the administration's lack of response to these attacks has deterred or emboldened our adversaries. The President recently announced a Cybersecurity National Action Plan. Whether this is too little too late, and the clarity of the overall guidance behind the plan, remains to be seen as we watch the most meaningful part of any grand plan: The execution. In this day in age, there is agreement that the battle for the security of our information systems is continually escalating. The testimony today will help inform what actions Congress can take to further the interests of our National security.

Mr. RATCLIFFE. The Chair now recognizes the Ranking Minority Member of the subcommittee, the gentleman from Louisiana, Mr. Richmond, for his opening statement.

Mr. RICHMOND. Thank you, Mr. Chairman, and thank you for holding this hearing today on information security threats and how we manage cyber threat intelligence, areas that are central to our subcommittee's oversight responsibilities.

I also want to thank our witnesses for their participation in today's hearing, and especially welcome Dr. Porche from Baton Rouge, Louisiana, for being with us today.

The Department of Homeland Security plays a fundamental role in the National effort to increase our collective cybersecurity, but it cannot achieve its mission without a foundation of voluntary partnerships with the critical infrastructure community. The information security industry and our Government are partners.

The privately-owned critical infrastructures that are everywhere in my district, including ports, energy and pipeline networks, chemical manufacturers, and refineries, ship and supply goods and raw materials to all parts of our country and are vital to the jobs and economic well-being of my part of the world.

When the cyber information security and network systems fail for these kind of sites, whether from a natural disaster or a man-made intrusion, everyone feels it. It is the National interest to safeguard such critical infrastructure and to make sure that there are adequate protections from cyber and information and data interruptions.

This subcommittee has oversight responsibilities for the Department's US–CERT and ICS–CERT teams that provide the foundation of the U.S. Government's approach to securing and safeguarding the resilience of civilian cyber and critical infrastructure essential services.

It will be necessary for this subcommittee to continue to do all we can to help DHS develop a workable National cyber protection strategy and framework for critical infrastructure entities and small and large businesses in order to protect our economy.

After this subcommittee and full committee passed important information-sharing legislation last year, the legislation found its way to the President's desk, where he signed the Cybersecurity Information-Sharing Act, or CISA, on December 18, 2015.

Today I hope to hear from our witnesses how the Department is doing with its new information-sharing authorities and challenges and how cyber and information-sharing security industries are expanding their collaboration with the Department as a result of that legislation.

It will be important to know how cybersecurity companies can continue to collaborate with the Department to help US–CERT and ICS–CERT serve as the center of our National integration, information sharing and collaborative analysis for domestic and global cyber threat intelligence.

Finally, I hope to find out from our witnesses how we can help further the ability of DHS's National Cybersecurity and Communications Integration Center, or NCCIC, to receive and analyze information at machine speed, an analysis component of getting a leg up on the ever-changing landscape and world-wide cyber threat intelligence.

So I look forward to today's hearing. Mr. Chairman, with that, I yield back.

[The statement of Mr. Richmond follows:]

STATEMENT OF RANKING MEMBER CEDRIC L. RICHMOND

FEBRUARY 25, 2016

The Department of Homeland Security plays a fundamental role in the National effort to increase our collective cybersecurity, but it cannot achieve its mission without a foundation of voluntary partnerships with the critical infrastructure community, the information security industry, and our Government partners.

The privately-owned critical infrastructures that are everywhere in my district, including—ports, energy and pipeline networks, chemical manufacturers, and refineries—ship and supply goods and raw materials to all parts of our country, and are vital to the jobs and economic well-being of my part of the world.

When the cyber information security and network systems fail for these kinds of sites, whether from a natural disaster or a man-made intrusion, everyone feels it. It is in the National interest to safeguard such critical infrastructure, and to make sure there are adequate protections from cyber and information and data interruptions.

This subcommittee has oversight responsibilities for the Department's US–CERT and ICS–CERT teams that provide the foundation of the U.S. Government's approach to securing and safeguarding the resilience of civilian cyber, and critical infrastructure essential services. It will be necessary for this subcommittee to continue to do all we can to help DHS develop a workable, National cyber protection strategy and framework for critical infrastructure entities, and small and large businesses, in order to protect our economy.

After this subcommittee and full committee passed important information-sharing legislation last year, that legislation found its way to the President's desk where he signed the Cybersecurity Information Sharing Act, or CISA, on December 18, 2015.

Today I hope to hear from our witnesses how the Department is doing with its new information-sharing authorities and challenges, and how cyber and information security industries are expanding their collaboration with the Department as a result of the legislation.

It will be important to know how cybersecurity companies can continue to collaborate with the Department to help US–CERT and ICS–CERT serve as the center of our National integration, information sharing, and collaborative analysis, for domestic and global cyber threat intelligence.

Finally, I hope to find out from our witnesses how we can help further the ability of the DHS's National Cybersecurity and Communications Integration Center, or NCCIC, to receive and analyze information at machine speed—an essential component of getting a leg-up on the ever-changing landscape of world-wide cyber threat intelligence.

Mr. RATCLIFFE. I thank the gentleman. Other Members of the committee are reminded that opening statements may be submitted for the record.

[The statement of Honorable Sheila Jackson Lee follows:]

STATEMENT OF HONORABLE SHEILA JACKSON LEE

FEBRUARY 25, 2016

Chairman Ratcliff and Ranking Member Richmond thank you for your bipartisan leadership in holding today's hearing on "Emerging Cyber Threats to the United States."

There are critical cybersecurity issues that our Nation must face to ensure the protection of critical infrastructure and vital computer communication networks.

I thank today's witnesses who will provide their expert opinion on the issue of cybersecurity and critical infrastructure:

- Mr. Frank Cilluffo, associate vice president & director, Center for Cyber and Homeland Security, The George Washington University.
- Ms. Jennifer Kolde, lead technical director, FireEye Threat Intelligence.
- Mr. Adam Bromwich, vice president, Symantec Security Technology and Response. Representing the Cyber Threat Alliance.
- Dr. Isaac Porche, senior engineer at the RAND Corporation, and associate director of the Forces and Logistics Program for the RAND Army Research Division.

Last year, this committee and Congress acted in a bipartisan manner to pass critical cybersecurity legislation that enhanced the ability of the Department of Homeland Security to work with the private sector and other Federal civilian departments on cyber threat information sharing capabilities. Enactment of these bills represents a significant moment for the Department's cybersecurity mission.

I supported this effort by offering several amendments that were adopted by the full committee for inclusion in the cybersecurity legislation we passed.

This committee in particular undertook significant efforts to bring the bills to passage, and on December 18, 2015, President Obama signed into law the Cybersecurity Information Sharing Act of 2015 (CISA).

The work the Homeland Security did and particularly the leadership of this subcommittee is designed to increase cybersecurity information sharing between the private sector and the Federal Government.

Among other things, it provides various protections to non-Federal entities that share cyber threat indicators or defensive measures with the Federal Government.

I am a strong believer in legislative due process for addressing the most complex issues of the digital communication age.

Vulnerabilities in computing products are the chief method used by data thieves or terrorist to breach computing systems.

Since 2005 to the present, the Privacy Rights Clearinghouse, reports that 895,886,345 records have been breached.

The entities and their customers who have fallen victim to data breaches range in size from small businesses to major corporations and Federal Government agencies, such as:

- The IRS—101,000—the agency block payments to data thieves who used stolen identity information from elsewhere to generate pins using stolen Social Security Numbers (date reported 2/10/2016)
- Scottrade lost over 4 million records (October 1, 2015)

- Excellus Blue Cross Blue Shield lost over 10 million patient records (September 10, 2015)
- Office of Personnel Management (OPM) lost over 21.5 million Government employee or former employee records (June 4, 2015)

Most reports include no details on the number of records breached or stolen.

There is no law that requires companies to report breaches, but there are laws that require reports to consumers when their personal information may have been lost or stolen.

The security of Nation's critical infrastructure is critical to our prosperity and the American way of life.

Critical infrastructure in the form of our Nation's electric utility grid, water treatment facilities, energy refining and delivery systems; financial system; and much more needs strong cybersecurity to protect against threats.

Cybersecurity threats from the earliest days of the modern computing age.

Microsoft in order to protect their computing products from cybersecurity threats began to routinely release of updates to their software products on what has become known as "Patch Tuesdays."

Identifying and closing vulnerabilities in software and firmware IS one important means of securing systems from threats.

The link between commercially-available computing devices and our Nation's critical infrastructure lies in the role of products in ensuring the proper maintenance and operation of critical infrastructure.

RANSOMWARE AND CRIMINALS

The latest threat from cyber criminals is ransomware.

Criminals find vulnerabilities in a computer or computing network and use it to introduce an encryption application that locks the data so the owner or user of a computer system cannot access it until a ransom is paid to criminals who then unlock the data.

There are now ransomware encryption tools that encrypt data that cannot be unencrypted not even by the thieves.

If criminals find a way into a computer or computer network they will exploit that vulnerability.

Portable computing devices like iPads, iPhones, and laptops are used every day to access, perform tasks, and maintain critical infrastructure.

The security of physical space, such as our Nation's critical infrastructure, is about to inherit many of the security vulnerabilities that plague cyber space; because of the introduction of the Internet of Things (IoT).

The threats posed to computing devices include viruses; worms; Trojan horses; botnet creation, capture, and exploitation; pharming; phishing; denial-of-service attacks; and ransomware threats intended to undermine the proper functioning of physical security that incorporates or relies upon computing devices.

There are a range of threats presented by unintended actions by insiders that include introducing devices into the work IoT environment that carry exploitable vulnerabilities that could be seized upon by opportunistic applications or technology that probe the environment for stray information to collect and report back to cloud services or networks hosted by data and financial thieves.

Physical security in era of IoT environments will present challenges because of the number, diversity, and fluidity of digital technology that will traverse physical spaces.

Another challenge will be the speed that devices will change; the ability or willingness of manufacturers or providers to update software on every type of IoT device and to what degree remote actor (such as criminals, nation/states, or intellectual property thieves) may be able to explore potential vulnerabilities in larger, more complex systems by using very simple IoT-enabled technology.

Businesses large and small will adopt IoT technology without hesitation because of the tremendous opportunities for cost savings.

Lowering electricity bills based on actual usage; smart light bulbs that reduce output or completely turn off when sensors in a space indicate that it is unoccupied; employee credentials that not only act as a time clock, but a location service while employees are at work; and sensors that regulate the function of everything from water coolers to elevators base on a "just in time delivery" of only what is needed and exactly when it is needed.

Innovation will move at unprecedented pace, as new physical designs for everyday consumables will be changed to work as a node in the IoT.

The same light bulb from the same manufacturer will now have a wireless interface that allows it to send and receive wireless communications.

The same is true for the fleet of vehicles large and small that are used by employees on or off the campuses of companies or organizations.

In this fast-paced environment, one of the important protections for digital communications may not be available either through design or due to the limited capacity of the IoT device.

Password protection may be unavailable for many passive IoT wireless devices and this may further challenge physical security.

Exploitation of weaknesses found in the poor, or inefficient design of software or IoT device security may facilitate broader discussions about its implications for physical vulnerabilities and security threats.

The IoT appears to be about to project the power of computing into physical space without much consideration for the totality of the vulnerabilities and threats that may be imposed on once controlled and secure environments.

There will be no barriers within the IoT that will preserve physical security of businesses, government, or personal spaces unless they are created through broad voluntary adoption of standards that work both in theory and practice to address real-world challenges to physical security, privacy, or confidentiality.

Why should the security and privacy of IoT technology matter to physical security?

Physical security relies upon control over who or what can enter or exit a defined area or space.

The challenge to physical security posed by the IoT is a lack of security over the wireless communication signals and/or devices that may enter or exit a space.

The following are incidents that foreshadow some of the challenges to physical security in a world dominated by the IoT.

Security professionals responsible for facilities that rely on industrial control systems should be aware of new paths that may be used to access networks to cause disruptions to threats posed by cyber attacks that can result in physical damage to equipment.

A light bulb exploit

In 2014, it was reported that a LiFX system of wifi remote-controlled light bulb designed to work with a smart phone had security vulnerability.

Sensors on light bulbs designed to operate in conjunction with a smart phone offered an opportunity for a breach of other systems.

The problem was discovered in the software application that translates commands from a device's operating system, in this case the command to a light bulb to turn on or off.

The request from the computer to turn on or off the light bulb also asked for any additional information that might be stored in its IoT components which allowed for insecure code to be downloaded onto the computing network.

IoT enabled intercom systems (baby monitoring technology)

In September 2015, 2 years after the first cybersecurity warning regarding the security vulnerability of baby monitoring technology, it was reported that 9 baby monitor models for top manufacturers remain vulnerable to hacking.

There are documented cases of monitors being breached, allowing unauthorized voice communication from hackers over the communication system, and external access to video live feeds from baby's rooms.

This issue is relevant, because many properties or facilities for critical infrastructure will use if not already widely using automated systems to monitor locations.

Compromise of physical security monitoring systems could be used to prevent detection of physical threats to critical infrastructure.

Physical security of vehicles is in question

In 2015, researchers gained remote access to a Jeep Cherokee and took control of physical functions such as climate control, windshield wipers, and the sound-system.

They could even turn off the engine while the vehicle was in motion. Automobile manufacturers, not just of the Jeep Cherokee, understood that the computing systems of their vehicles could be compromised and took action to close the cybersecurity risk that had consequences for the physical security of their vehicles and the safety of their customers.

I held a staff briefing to bring this issue to the attention of the House and key Committees.

Physical security of industrial control systems

In 2010, Stuxnet—roughly 500 kilobytes of code—became known to computer security experts in the United States who identified it as a hybrid computer-worm designed to destroy physical equipment.

According to a September 2010 Symantic report, there were 100,000 Stuxnet-infected computers world-wide.

Stuxnet moved from system to system through connected and unconnected computing technology using the Microsoft Windows Operating System.

If a machine was not connected to a network, sticking a USB drive into an infected machine, then into the uninfected machine was sufficient for Stuxnet to spread. Once Stuxnet is inside of a machine or network, it replicates itself.

In 2012, the United States Government started to warn of a "Cyber Pearl Harbor."

Stuxnet is not limited to harming the function of gas centrifuges used to enrich uranium, but can damage or destroy machines or equipment controlled by industrial control systems used for a range of non-military purposes.

The capacity of Stuxnet to destroy equipment or make it unusable poses a threat to physical security.

Another cyber threat is the Flame worm, which appears to have been introduced through an update to Microsoft's Windows 7 operating system, which is phenomenal because to get Windows Operating system to accept an update it has to authenticate that the request source of the update is coming from the company.

Stuxnet or Flame worms can be altered to attack a wide range of industrial control systems or critical infrastructure.

Stuxnet-derived worm code could be written to damage water treatment and delivery systems, electricity delivery systems, industrial control systems used by food processors, ports operations, or automobile assembly lines.

Laying the ground work for seeking out vulnerabilities to exploit and therefore to defend, Hungarian researchers in September 2011 uncovered "Duqu" a program that was designed to steal data regarding industrial control systems.

What will be the IoT physical security challenges of complex operations?

The security of deep-water and container ports have been wedded from their earliest beginnings because cargo was personal wealth and nation-state commerce.

The volume of activity at deep-water and container ports made innovation and computing necessary for automation of facilities to management port functions.

However, no one system manages everything that happens at deep-water and container ports. Arrivals and departures may be managed by one system; loading and offloading by another entity; container management by another provider; employee access by another system, and private companies may track their cargo using proprietary systems.

The number, type, and severity of cyber threats experienced by ports, service providers, or port customers are unknown.

The preference is not to report incidents and to payor absorb costs resulting from breaches or thefts.

The other reasons for underreporting is likely that companies and ports are unaware that their cybersecurity has been breached.

An October 15, 2014, report by CyberKeel entitled, "Maritime Cyber-Risks", reported on financial thefts; alteration of carrier information regarding cargo location; barcode scanners use as hacking devices (a variation of the light bulb vulnerability described above); targeting of shipbuilding and maritime operations; cyber-enabled large drug-smuggling operations; compromising of Australian Custom and Border protection; spoofing a vessel Automated Identification System (AIS); drilling rig cyber attack; vessel navigation control hack; GPS jamming; vulnerabilities in the Electronic Chart Display and Information System; and a Danish Maritime Authority breach.

Deletion of carrier information

In August 2011, an incident of deletion of carrier information regarding the location of cargo occurred against the Islamic Republic of Iran Shipping Lines. The attack damaged all the data related to cargo ship contents, which meant that no one knew where any containers were or the status of containers—off-loaded, picked up, or still on board ships. The data was eventually recovered, but the disruption in operation of the business was significant.

Barcode scanner hacking tool

The attack was named "Zombie Zero" and involved malware hidden in the software for barcode scanners of at least 8 different companies.

The malware activated when the barcode readers were connected to company networks. When connected, the malware launched a series of automated attacks searching for the location of the financial server.

Upon location of the financial server, the malware would compromise the target server to be taken over.

Australian customs exploit

A cyber-crime organization breached the cargo system of Australian Customs and Border Protection, which allowed criminals to verify that their shipping containers were viewed as suspicious by the police or customs authorities.

This allowed criminals to abandon contraband that would result in arrests or confiscation and focus on what they knew would be released without difficulty.

Drilling rig cyber attack

In 2010, while a drilling rig was being moved from the construction site in South Korea toward South America, its critical control systems were infected by malware that shut it down for 19 days to fix the problem.

A similar attack on a rig reported off the coast of Africa caused it to be shut down for a week.

These are some of the critical cybersecurity threats facing critical infrastructure. I look forward to the testimony of today's witnesses.

Thank you.

Mr. RATCLIFFE. We are pleased to have a distinguished panel of witnesses before us today on this very important topic. Joining us, our first witness is Mr. Frank Cilluffo, who is the associate vice president and director of the George Washington University Center for Cyber and Homeland Security. Welcome, Mr. Cilluffo.

Also with us is Ms. Jennifer Kolde. She is the lead technical director for FireEye Threat Intelligence. Thanks for being here today.

Mr. Adam Bromwich is the vice president for security technology and response at Symantec and is also representing the cyber threat alliance. Welcome, Mr. Bromwich.

Finally, last but not least, Dr. Isaac Porche—did I say that correctly—is the associate director of the Forces and Logistics Program within Army Research Division of the RAND Corporation. Welcome, Doctor.

I would now ask the witnesses all to stand and raise your right hand, and I will swear you in to give your testimony.

[Witnesses sworn.]

Let the record reflect that the witnesses have all answered in the affirmative. The witnesses' full written statements will appear in the record. The Chair now recognizes Mr. Cilluffo for his opening statement.

STATEMENT OF FRANK J. CILLUFFO, ASSOCIATE VICE PRESIDENT AND DIRECTOR, CENTER FOR CYBER AND HOMELAND SECURITY, THE GEORGE WASHINGTON UNIVERSITY

Mr. CILLUFFO. Chairman Ratcliffe, Ranking Member Richmond, Congressmen Marino and Donovan, thank you for the opportunity to testify before you today.

Mr. Chairman, I think you did an amazing job framing the issues here, so I will try to be even more brief, which is not my strong suit, since I have never had an unspoken thought, but I will try to hit on a couple points that weren't addressed.

I mean, obviously today the United States faces a dizzying array of cyber threats from many and varied actors. Virtually every day, there is a new incident in the headlines, and the initiative clearly remains with the attacker. As you mentioned, Mr. Chairman, last week, it was Hollywood Presbyterian.

Also last week, there was some news of a manipulation, a Russian hack that took place about a year ago where they were able to manipulate the U.S. dollar and ruble exchange rate. Even more disconcerting was the December 2015 cyber attack on Ukraine's electric grid, which affected 4 dozen substations and left a quarter million people without power.

At the same time as the attack on the grid itself, call centers were hit with a telephony denial-of-service attack as customers were trying to report the outages. So if anyone thought this was a glitch, think again.

U.S. critical infrastructure, notably lifeline sectors such as energy and electricity, telecommunications, transportation, water, and financial services from banks to exchanges and clearinghouses are in the crosshairs and are primary targets for cyber attacks and cyber crimes. Our National security, public safety, economic competitiveness, and personal privacy are at risk.

The threat tempo is magnified by the speed at which technologies continue to evolve and by the fact that our adversaries continue to adapt their tactics, techniques, and procedures in order to evade and defeat the latest prevention and response measures.

While breaches to date have largely exemplified data theft and destruction, a concerning trend looking ahead will be data manipulation. A few words on the threat itself, and I hope there will be some time during Q&A to expand.

First, not all hacks are the same, nor are all hackers the same. The threat comes in various shapes, sizes, and forms, ranging from nation-states at the high end of the threat spectrum to foreign terrorist organizations, criminal enterprises, and hacktivists. Just as diverse as the threat actors themselves are the intentions, capabilities, and TTPs, or tactics, techniques, and procedures, and the tools they ultimately utilize.

Put another way, nearly every form of conflict today and tomorrow will have a cyber dimension to it. Whereas technologies will continue to evolve and change, human nature remains pretty consistent. If it happens in the physical world, it is happening in the cyber world, and increasingly you are seeing those two worlds converge, especially with the advent of the Internet of Things and Internet of Everything.

A couple of quick top-line words on the threat actors. As I just mentioned, nation-state and their proxies continue to present the greatest and most advanced and persistent threat in the cyber domain. My testimony will focus on 4 key actors, all of which, Mr. Chairman, you identified. But it is important to keep in mind the broader context.

Every country that has a modern military and intelligence service also has a computer network attack capability. Topping the list are countries that are integrating computer network attack and computer network exploit into their warfighting strategy and doctrine. The most sophisticated actors are obviously Russia and China.

Nation-states often use proxies to conceal their involvement. In turn, there are different grades of proxies. They may be state-sanctioned, state-sponsored, or state-supported. While improvements have been made in terms of attribution, we are by no means at the place where we hope and need to be.

Both China and Russia are known to use proxies to do their bidding, largely to provide plausible deniability. After these 2 countries come Iran and North Korea. While as you mentioned, Mr. Chairman, they are not up to par with Russia and China in terms of their capability, they are investing very heavily in their computer network attack capabilities. What they may lack in capability, unfortunately, they make up for in intent.

Moreover, having fewer constraints, then you are starting to see more concern that they are turned to attack, not just espionage, and this is evidenced by the 2013 DDOS attacks on the U.S. banks, by the Sands Casino attack, by the Saudi Aramco and Qatari RasGas attacks, just to name a few, and North Korea's attacks on South Korean banks, energy companies, and, of course, Sony.

Next up were foreign terrorist organizations. They certainly possess the motivation and intent, but fortunately they do not have the same level of capability that nations do, in terms of cyber means. But the recent doxing attacks and tactics used against U.S. military and law enforcement is troubling and indicative of an emerging threat.

It is likely that ISIS or their sympathizers will increasingly turn to disruptive cyber attacks. What capabilities they don't possess they can simply buy or rent, as cyber weapons are readily available and accessible in the deep web and dark net. Think cyber drive-by shootings—they may not have a sustained capability, but they can have a disruptive capability.

By contrast, criminal organizations and criminal enterprises possess substantial capabilities, but obviously their motivation and intent differs from terrorists. They don't want to bring attention to their cause. They are in it for what? They are in it for money, so by and large they are going to be the most quiet and subtle actors in the cyber domain.

However, it is disconcerting when you look at some of the trends where criminal enterprises are working increasingly with nation-states, notably Russia.

In closing, while I recognize the focus of the hearing is on cyber threats, I do want to say a couple words on recommendations going forward. From the standpoint of critical infrastructure, a sustained campaign of cyber attacks hold the potential to undermine trust and confidence in the system itself, irrespective of the perpetrator.

How many companies, even the largest, went into business thinking they were defending themselves against foreign intelligence services? That is precisely what is happening today, companies taking on nations or being exploited by nations.

We need to impose costs for bad cyber behavior on those who are currently acting with impunity. This demands articulating and more importantly demonstrating a cyber deterrence strategy. Second, cyber crime is the only crime I know of where we blame the victim. Yes, companies can do and must do more to shore up their cybersecurity, but the current approach or business as usual is doomed for failure, as it is completely reactive.

If you think about it, every time we get hit or breached, it is the equivalent of calling a locksmith, not a police officer, the locksmith. We can't simply react and continue to build higher walls or bigger locks.

Moving forward, in connection with this last point, the U.S. Government must give companies who now find themselves at the tip of the spear, the framework, parameters, and tools that they need in order to engage in active defense to protect themselves and their customers.

Thank you, Mr. Chairman, and sorry for going a little over.

[The prepared statement of Mr. Cilluffo follows:]

PREPARED STATEMENT OF FRANK J. CILLUFFO

FEBRUARY 25, 2016

Chairman Ratcliffe, Ranking Member Richmond, and distinguished subcommittee Members, thank you for this opportunity to testify before you today. The United States currently faces an almost dizzying array of cyber threats from many and varied actors. Virtually every day there is a new incident in the headlines and the initiative clearly remains with the attacker. Critical infrastructure, such as the U.S. financial services sector, is in the crosshairs as a primary target; but our banks are not alone—"lifeline" sectors such as energy & electricity, telecommunications, transportation, and water are similarly situated. According to the Department of Homeland Security, cyber attacks on U.S. industrial control systems rose 20 percent last year as compared to the year before, with the energy sector among those hardest hit.[1] Just days ago, hackers took a Los Angeles hospital off-line, demanding ransom in bitcoins to restore systems and operations.[2] And no one is immune from digital targeting of crucial infrastructure: earlier this month for instance, it was reported that hackers "used malware to infiltrate a Russian regional bank and manipulate the ruble-dollar exchange rate by more than 15 percent in minutes."[3]

The threat tempo is magnified by the speed at which technologies continue to evolve and by the fact that our adversaries continue to adapt their tactics, techniques and procedures in order to evade and defeat our prevention and response measures. While breaches to date have largely exemplified data theft, the next step that hostile actors take may go further—such as data manipulation. Just imagine the havoc that a creative adversary could wreak this way, by changing our most sensitive and private information, with everything from medical records to stock exchanges potentially at risk. Against this background, a strong detection and mitigation program is just as necessary as a strong defense. While it is important to continue to invest in technologies and procedures to prevent attacks, the reality is that nobody can prevent all attacks; but significant steps can be taken to minimize the impact and consequences of an attack. This posture, one of substantial resilience, must also extend to our partners in the private sector, which own and operate 85 percent of U.S. critical infrastructure.

At the National level, the challenge is to understand as best we can the threat as it manifests in so many different incarnations; and to prioritize it so that our limited resources for preventing and containing the challenge are directed as efficiently and effectively as possible. This includes supporting the private sector which now finds itself on the front lines, so as to allow U.S. businesses to engage in active defense of their "crown jewels"—from trade secrets to R&D-related intellectual property and so on.

Taking a global perspective on cyber threats, the bottom line up front is as follows:

---

[1] U.S. Department of Homeland Security, *ICS CERT Monitor*, November/December 2015. *https://ics-cert.us-cert.gov/sites/default/files/Monitors/ICS-CERT%20Monitor_Nov-Dec2015-S508C.pdf*.

[2] Brian Barrett, "Hack Brief: Hackers Are Holding an L.A. Hospital's Computers Hostage," *Wired*, Feb. 2, 2016. *http://www.wired.com/2016/02/hack-brief-hackers-are-holding-an-la-hospitals-computers-hostage/*.

[3] Katie Bo Williams, "Report: Hackers use Malware to Manipulate Russian Currency Value," *The Hill*, Feb. 8, 2016. *http://thehill.com/policy/cybersecurity/268588-report-hackers-use-malware-to-manipulate-russian-currency-value*.

- The threat spectrum includes a wide array of actors with different intentions, motivations, and capabilities.
- Nation-states and their proxies continue to present the greatest—meaning most advanced and persistent—threat in the cyber domain. This testimony will focus on four key threat actors, but it is important to keep in mind the broader context: every country that has a modern military and intelligence service also has a computer network attack capability.[4] Importantly, nation-states vary in terms of both their capability and intent, with some being more willing to exercise their cyber capabilities than others.
- Nation-states often use proxies to conceal state involvement. In turn, there are different grades of proxies: They may be state-sanctioned, state-sponsored, or state-supported.
- Foreign terrorist organizations certainly possess the motivation and intent but fortunately, they have yet to fully develop a sustained cyber attack capability. Recent "doxing" tactics against U.S. military and law enforcement personnel by the Islamic State in Iraq and Syria (ISIS) is troubling and indicative of an emerging threat. It is likely that ISIS, or their sympathizers, will increasingly turn to disruptive cyber attacks.
- By contrast, criminal organizations possess substantial capabilities, but their motivation and intent differs from terrorists. Rather than being motivated by ideology or political concerns, criminal organizations are driven by the profit motive. However criminals are increasingly working with or for nation-states such as Russia; and this convergence of forces heightens the dangers posed by both groups.
- Yet other entities such as "hacktivists" may also possess considerable skills and abilities; and when their special interests or core concerns are perceived to be in play, these individuals can be a significant disruptive force whether acting alone or loosely in tandem, essentially as a leaderless movement. Their motive is often to cause maximum embarrassment to their targets and to bring attention to their cause.
- Regardless of actor, there are many different modalities of attack. Tactics, techniques, and procedures include malware, exploitation of zero-day vulnerabilities, distributed denial-of-service (DDoS) attacks, and the use of botnets. Data may be stolen or manipulated. The use of ransomware and crypto-ransomware is also on the rise: Hospitals, police departments, and schools have been hit. For a good overview of these trends, see Symantec's 2015 *Internet Security Threat Report.*[5]
- In reference to any threat vector, a worst-case scenario would combine kinetic and cyber attacks; and the cyber component would serve as a force multiplier to increase the lethality or impact of the physical attack.
- The insider threat also cuts across vectors and can materialize within any actor, from the nation-state on down.
- Finally, critical infrastructure such as U.S. banks and the energy sector (oil & gas) are primary targets for cyber attacks and cyber crimes. A concerted campaign against these crucial infrastructures holds the potential to undermine trust and confidence in the system itself, irrespective of the perpetrator. Below the various categories of actors are examined in greater detail in terms of the nature of the threat they pose and how they function.

NATION-STATES

The most advanced and persistent cyber threats to the United States today remain nation-states and their proxies, and in particular China and Russia. In addition, Iran has increased its cyber capabilities exponentially in recent years. And with the hack of Sony Corporation—which made use of more than half a dozen exploits lest the target be patched against one or more of these vulnerabilities, North Korea too has demonstrated itself to be a significant adversary.

---

[4] Over 100 governments have stood up military entities to engage in cyber warfare, according to Peter Singer and Allan Friedman ("Cybersecurity and Cyberwar: What Everyone Needs to Know," *Oxford University Press*, Jan. 3, 2014). The *Wall Street Journal* recently reported that "29 countries have formal military or intelligence units dedicated to offensive hacking," out of 60 that are developing tools for computer-enabled espionage or attacks (Damian Paletta, Danny Yadron, and Jennifer Valentino-Devries, "Cyberwar Ignites a New Arms Race," *Wall Street Journal*, Oct. 11, 2015). Discrepancies in these numbers are due to varying definitions of cyber warfare units, but the underlying point that there are a number of cyber-capable state actors is clear.

[5] "Internet Security Threat Report, Volume 20," *Symantec*, April 2015.

Against the growing abilities of these key threat actors for "on-line espionage, disinformation, theft, propaganda, and data-destruction,"[6] the Director of National Intelligence James Clapper recently observed (during the annual world-wide threat assessment offered to Congress earlier this month) that, "improving offensive tradecraft, the use of proxies, and the creation of cover organizations will hinder timely, high-confidence attribution of responsibility for state-sponsored cyber operations."[7] This is significant because the harder it is to attribute activity, the harder it is to deter and punish the perpetrator.

How do these actors function?

Our adversaries have engaged in brazen activity, from computer network exploitation (CNE) to computer network attack (CNA). CNE includes traditional, economic, and industrial espionage, as well as intelligence preparation of the battlefield (IPB)—such as surveillance and reconnaissance of attack targets, and the mapping of critical infrastructures for potential future targeting in a strategic campaign. In turn, CNA encompasses activities that alter (disrupt, destroy, etc.) the targeted data/information. The line between CNE and CNA is thin, however: If one can exploit, one can also attack if the intent exists to do so.

Foreign militaries are, increasingly, integrating CNE and CNA capabilities into their warfighting and military planning and doctrine, as well as their grand strategy. These efforts may allow our adversaries to enhance their own weapon systems and platforms, as well as stymie those of others. Moreover, CNAs may occur simultaneously with other forms of attack (kinetic, insider threats, etc.).

Our adversaries are also interweaving the cyber domain into the activities of their foreign intelligence services, to include intelligence derived from human sources (HUMINT).

This said our adversaries are certainly not all of a piece. Rather, nation-states may differ from one another, or from their proxies, in their motivation and intent. Tradecraft and its application may also differ widely. From a U.S. perspective, the challenge is to parse our understanding of key actors and their particular behaviors, factoring details about each threat vector into a tailored U.S. response that is designed to dissuade, deter, and compel.[8]

China

China possesses sophisticated cyber capabilities and has demonstrated a striking level of perseverance, evidenced by the sheer number of attacks and acts of espionage that the country commits. Reports of the Office of the U.S. National Counterintelligence Executive have called out China and its cyber espionage, characterizing these activities as rising to the level of strategic threat to the U.S. National interest.[9]

The U.S.-China Economic and Security Review Commission notes further: "Computer network operations have become fundamental to the PLA's strategic campaign goals for seizing information dominance early in a military operation."[10]

China's aggressive collection efforts appear to be intended to amass data and secrets (military, commercial/proprietary, etc.) that will support and further the country's economic growth, scientific, and technological capacities, military power, etc.—all with an eye to securing strategic advantage in relation to (perceived or actual) competitor countries and adversaries.

In May 2015, data theft on a massive scale, affecting virtually all U.S. Government employees, was traced back to China. Whether the hack was state-sponsored, state-supported, or simply tolerated through a blind eye by the government of China, is not yet clear. But military officers in China are increasingly known to moonlight as hackers for hire when off the clock; and countries are increasingly

---

[6] Spencer Ackerman and Sam Thielman, "US Intelligence Chief: We Might Use the Internet of Things to Spy on You," *The Guardian*, Feb. 9, 2016. *http://www.theguardian.com/technology/2016/feb/09/internet-of-things-smart-home-devices-government-surveillance-james-clapper.*

[7] James R. Clapper, Director of National Intelligence, Statement for the Record, "Worldwide Threat Assessment of the U.S. Intelligence Community," Senate Armed Services Committee, Feb. 9, 2016.

[8] Frank J. Cilluffo and Rhea D. Siers, "Cyber Deterrence is a Strategic Imperative," *Wall Street Journal*, Apr. 28, 2015. *http://blogs.wsj.com/cio/2015/04/28/cyber-deterrence-is-a-strategic-imperative/.*

[9] Foreign Spies Stealing U.S. Economic Secrets in Cyberspace, *Report to Congress on Foreign Economic Collection and Industrial Espionage, 2009–2011*, Oct. 2011. *http://www.ncix.gov/publications/reports/fecie_all/Foreign_Economic_Collection_2011.pdf.*

[10] *http://www.uscc.gov/RFP/2012/USCC%20Report_Chinese_CapabilitiesforComputer_-NetworkOperationsandCyberEspionage.pdf.*

turning to proxies do their bidding in order to provide plausible deniability.[11] The extent to which China may benefit from the massive data breach such as by using the information to blackmail and recruit Americans thus remains to be seen.

In September 2015, China and the United States reached an agreement on refraining from conducting economic cyber-espionage. Earlier this month, DNI Clapper noted that there is evidence of "limited on-going cyber activity from China", but as yet it has not been confirmed to be state-sponsored. Mean time however, China appears to be giving "security and intelligence agencies a larger role in helping Beijing hack foreign companies."[12]

Russia

Russia's cyber capabilities are, arguably, even more sophisticated than those of China, and Russia has been particularly adept at integrating cyber into its strategic plans and operations.[13] The Office of the U.S. National Counterintelligence Executive (NCIX) observes: "Moscow's highly capable intelligence services are using HUMINT, cyber, and other operations to collect economic information and technology to support Russia's economic development and security. Russia's extensive attacks on U.S. research and development have resulted in Russia being deemed (along with China), "a national long-term strategic threat to the United States," by the NCIX.[14] Also concerning, Russia and China recently signed a cybersecurity agreement pursuant to which they pledge not to hack one another and to share both information and technology.[15]

In 2009, the *Wall Street Journal* reported that cyber spies from Russia and China had penetrated the U.S. electrical grid, leaving behind software programs. The intruders did not cause damage to U.S. infrastructure, but sought to navigate the systems and their controls. Was this reconnaissance or an act of aggression? What purpose could the mapping of critical U.S. infrastructure serve, other than intelligence preparation of the battlefield? The NASDAQ exchange, too, has allegedly been the target of a "complex hack" by a nation-state. Again, one questions the motivation.[16]

More recently, Russian hackers believed to be doing their government's bidding breached the White House, the State Department, and the Defense Department.[17] Similar forces were also poised to cyber-attack U.S. banks against the backdrop of economic sanctions levied against Russia for its repeated and brazen incursions into Ukraine.[18]

Russia has also engaged in cyber operations against Ukraine (2014/15), Georgia (2008), and Estonia (2007); in the first 2 instances combining them with kinetic operations. Notably, in December 2015, western Ukraine experienced a power outage that is believed to have been caused by cyber attack perpetrated by Russia. Though one power company reported the incident, "similar malware was found in the networks of at least 2 other utilities."[19] More than 4 dozen substations were affected,

---

[11] Sharon L. Cardash and Frank J. Cilluffo, "Massive Government Employee Data Theft Further Complicates US-China Relations," *The Conversation*, June 8, 2015. *https://theconversation.com/massive-government-employee-data-theft-further-complicates-us-china-relations-42941*; and Kelly Jackson Higgins, "State-Owned Chinese Firms Hired Military hackers for IT Services," *Dark Reading*, May 21, 2014. *http://www.darkreading.com/attacks-breaches/state-owned-chinese-firms-hired-military-hackers-for-it-services/d/d-id/1269102*.

[12] Jack Detsch, "Report: China Bolsters State Hacking Powers," *Christian Science Monitor—Passcode*, Feb. 4, 2016. *http://www.csmonitor.com/World/Passcode/2016/0204/Report-China-bolsters-state-hacking-powers*.

[13] Jason Wirtz, "Cyber War and Strategic Culture: The Russian Integration of Cyber Power into Grand Strategy," NATO Cooperative Cyber Defence Center of Excellence, 2015.

[14] *http://www.ncix.gov/publications/reports/fecie_all/Foreign_Economic_Collection_20-11.pdf*.

[15] Cory Bennett, "Russia, China Unite with Major Cyber Pact," *The Hill*, May 8, 2015. *http://thehill.com/policy/cybersecurity/241453-russia-china-unit-with-major-cyber-pact*.

[16] *http://www.bloomberg.com/bw/articles/2014-07-17/how-russian-hackers-stole-the-nasdaq*.

[17] Evan Perez and Shimon Prokupecz, "How the U.S. Thinks Russians Hacked the White House," *CNN*, Apr. 8, 2015, *http://www.cnn.com/2015/04/07/politics/how-russians-hacked-the-wh/*; and Cory Bennett, "Defense chief: Russian goals in Pentagon hack 'not clear'," *The Hill*, May 15, 2015, *http://thehill.com/policy/cybersecurity/242213-pentagon-head-russian-goals-not-clear-in-dod-hack*.

[18] Cory Bennett, "Russian Hacking Group was Set to hit U.S. Banks," *The Hill*, May 13, 2015 *http://thehill.com/policy/rsecurity/241965-russian-hacking-group-was-set-to-hit-us-banks*; and "APT28: A Window into Russia's Cyber Espionage Operations?" *FireEye*, October 27, 2015 *https://www.fireeye.com/blog/threat-research/2014/10/apt28-a-window-into-russias-cyber-espionage-operations.html*; and Frank J. Cilluffo and Sharon L. Cardash, "How to Stop Putin Hacking the White House," *Newsweek*, April 13, 2015, *http://www.newsweek.com/how-stop-putin-hacking-white-house-321857*; and *http://www.cnbc.com/id/102025262*.

[19] Eric Auchard and Jim Finkle, "Experts: Ukraine Utility Cyberattack Wider than Reported," *Reuters*, January 4, 2016. *http://m.voanews.com/a/reu-experts-ukraine-utility-cyberattack-wider-than-reported/3131554.html*.

as were more than a quarter of a million customers for up to 6 hours. In addition, a simultaneous attack on call centers (a telephony denial of service attack) hindered communication and customer reporting of difficulties. The case is truly significant: It is believed to represent the first time that a blackout was caused by computer network attack.

Over time, Russia's history has also demonstrated a toxic blend of crime, business, and politics—and there are few, if any, signs that things are changing today. To the contrary, a convergence between the Russian intelligence community and cyber criminals has been observed as relations between Russia and the West have deterio-rated as the conflict over Ukraine has unfolded.[20] Evidence of the complicity be-tween the Russian government and its cyber criminals and hackers became even starker when the Russian Foreign Ministry issued "a public notice advising 'citizens to refrain from traveling abroad, especially to countries that have signed agree-ments with the U.S. on mutual extradition, if there is reasonable suspicion that U.S. law enforcement agencies' have a case pending against them."[21]

Notably the DNI stated to Congress this month that Russia is "assuming a more assertive cyber posture based on its willingness to target critical infrastructure sys-tems and conduct espionage operations even when detected."[22] It has also been re-ported that Russia's Defense Ministry is standing up a cyber command which will "be responsible for conducting offensive cyber activities, including propaganda oper-ations and inserting malware into enemy command and control systems."[23]

Iran

Iran has invested heavily in recent years to deepen and expand its cyber warfare capacity. Under President Rouhani, the country's cybersecurity budget has in-creased "twelve-fold"; and the country may now be considered "a top-five world cyber power."[24]

This concerted effort and the associated rapid rise through the ranks comes in the wake of the Stuxnet worm, which targeted Iran's nuclear weapons development pro-gram. How the recently concluded international agreement on containing that pro-gram will affect Iran's behavior in the cyber domain over the long run remains to be seen—although early reports indicate that Iran "has ramped up its cyber espio-nage, targeting . . . the emails and social media accounts of State Department offi-cials whose work is related to Iran and the Middle East."[25] Another important but open question is whether and how recent reports that the United States had formu-lated plans to disable Iran's nuclear program by cyber means, in the event that nu-clear negotiations failed and military conflict ensued, may affect Iran's cyber-behav-ior moving forward.[26]

We also know that Iran has engaged in a concerted cyber campaign against U.S. banks.[27] In January 2013, the *Wall Street Journal* reported [28] on "an intensifying

[20] John Leyden, "Ukraine Conflict Spilling Over into Cyber-crime, Warns Former Spy Boss," *The Register*, April 16, 2015. *http://www.theregister.co.uk/2015/04/16/cyber_war_key-note_infiltrate/*.

[21] Kevin Poulsen, "Russia Issues International Travel Advisory to its Hackers," *Wired*, Sep-tember 3, 2013. *http://www.wired.com/2013/09/dont-leave-home/*.

[22] James R. Clapper, Director of National Intelligence, "Worldwide Threat Assessment of the US Intelligence Community," Statement for the Record before the U.S. Senate, Armed Services Committee, February 9, 2016. *http://www.dni.gov/files/documents/SASC_Unclassified_-2016_ATA_SFR_FINAL.pdf*.

[23] James R. Clapper, Director of National Intelligence, "Worldwide Cyber Threats," Statement for the Record before The U.S. House of Representatives, Permanent Select Committee on Intel-ligence, September 10, 2015. *http://docs.house.gov/meetings/IG/IG00/20150910/103797/HHRG-114-IG00-Wstate-ClapperJ-20150910.PDF*.

[24] Cory Bennett, "Iran has Boosted Cyber Spending Twelvefold," *The Hill*, March 23, 2015. *http://thehill.com/policy/cybersecurity/236627-iranian-leader-has-boosted-cyber-spending-12-fold*.

[25] Cory Bennett, "Iran Launches Cyber Offensive after Nuclear Deal," *The Hill*, November 24, 2015. *http://thehill.com/policy/cybersecurity/261190-iran-switches-to-cyber-espionage-after-nu-clear-deal*.

[26] David Sanger and Mark Mazetti, "U.S. Had Cyberattack Plan if Iran Nuclear Dispute Led to Conflict," *The New York Times*, February 16, 2016. *http://.nytimes.com/2016/02/17/world/middleast/us-had-cyberattack-planned-if-iran-nuclear-negotiations-failed.html?smid=nytcore-iphone-share&smprod=nytcore-iphone*.

[27] Shane Harris, "Forget China: Iran's Hackers are America's Newest Cyber Threat," *Foreign Policy*, February 18, 2014. *http://foreignpolicy.com/2014/02/18/forget-china-irans-hackers-are-americas-newest-cyber-threat/*.

[28] Siobhan Gorman and Danny Yadron, "Banks Seek U.S. Help on Iran Cyberattacks," *The Wall Street Journal*, January 16, 2013. *http://www.wsj.com/articles/SB10001424127-887324734904578244302923178548*.

Iranian campaign of cyber attacks [thought to have begun months earlier] against American financial institutions" including Bank of America, PNC Financial Services Group, Sun Trust Banks Inc., and BB&T Corp. Six leading U.S. banks—including J.P. Morgan Chase—were targeted in "the most disruptive" wave of this campaign, characterized by DDoS attacks. The Izz ad-Din al-Qassam Cyber Fighters claim responsibility for all of these incidents.

U.S. officials also believe Iran to be responsible for a cyber attack against the Sands Casino in Las Vegas owned by politically active billionaire Sheldon Adelson. The incident appears to be a first: "a foreign player simply sought to destroy American corporate infrastructure on such a scale . . . PCs and servers were shut . . . down in a cascading IT catastrophe, with many of their hard drives wiped clean."[29]

Iran has also long relied on proxies such as Hezbollah—which now has a companion organization called Cyber Hezbollah—to strike at perceived adversaries. Iran and Hezbollah are suspected in connection with the August 2012 cyber attacks on the state-owned oil company Saudi Aramco and on Qatari producer RasGas, which resulted in the compromise of approximately 30,000 computers.[30]

In addition, elements of Iran's Revolutionary Guard Corps (IRGC) have also openly sought to pull hackers into the fold, including the political/criminal hacker group Ashiyane; and the Basij, who are paid to do cyber work on behalf of the regime.[31]

North Korea (DPRK)

As perhaps the world's most isolated state-actor in the international system, North Korea operates under fewer constraints. For this reason, the country poses an important "wildcard" threat, not only to the United States but also to the region and to broader international stability.

South Korea's Defense Ministry estimates that North Korea possesses a force of "about 6,000 cyber agents."[32] A frequent DPRK target, South Korea has attributed a series of cyber attacks—upon its Hydro & Nuclear Power Company (2014) and upon its banks and broadcasting companies (2013), for example—to North Korea.[33]

From a U.S. standpoint, it is the North Korean attack on Sony Pictures Entertainment late last year that looms large: "'There was disruption. There was destruction of data. There was an intent to hurt the company. And it succeeded, bringing a major U.S. entertainment company to its knees.'"[34]

Where will the DPRK go from here? In the words of an Australian expert, "There's growing concern amongst analysts, and government officials alike that North Korea has begun to rapidly accelerate its development of advanced offensive cyber capabilities'."[35] This concern is compounded by the fact that, potentially, "cyber operations . . . could be integrated in the future with a military strategy designed to disrupt U.S. systems."[36]

These developments are all the more disturbing when considered in tandem with the following trenchant question raised by one of my CCHS colleagues: "'Given North Korea's proclivity to provide other destructive technologies and military as-

---

[29] Ben Elgin and Michael Riley, "Now at the Sands Casino: An Iranian hacker in Every Server," *Bloomberg Business*, December 11, 2015. *http://www.bloomberg.com/bw/articles/2014-12-11/iranian-hackers-hit-sheldon-adelsons-sands-casino-in-las-vegas.*

[30] Kim Zetter, "The NSA Acknowledges What we all Feared: Iran Learns from US Cyberattacks," *Wired*, February 10, 2015. *http://www.wired.com/2015/02/nsa-acknowledges-feared-iran-learns-us-cyberattacks/.*

[31] Frank J. Cilluffo, "The Iranian Cyber Threat to the United States," Testimony before the U.S. House of Representatives, Committee on Homeland Security, Subcommittee on Counterterrorism and Intelligence and Subcommittee on Cybersecurity, Infrastructure Protection, and Security Technologies, April 26, 2012. *http://cchs.gwu.edu/sites/cchs.gwu.edu/files/downloads/Testimony_Cilluffo_April_26_2012.pdf.*

[32] Leo Byrne, "N. Korean Hacking Threat Leads to Blue House Cyber-security Office," *NK News*, March 31, 2015. *http://www.nknews.org/2015/03/n-korean-hacking-threat-leads-to-blue-house-cyber-security-office/.*

[33] Tae-jun Kang, "South Korea Beefs up Cyber Security with an Eye on North Korea," *The Diplomat*, April 1, 2015. *http://thediplomat.com/2015/04/south-korea-beefs-up-cyber-security-with-an-eye-on-north-korea/.*

[34] James Lewis, "The Attack on Sony," *CBS News 60 Minutes*, April 12, 2015. *http://www.cbsnews.com/news/north-korean-cyberattack-on-sony-60-minutes/.*

[35] Leo Byrne, "N. Korean Hacking Threat Leads to Blue House Cyber-security Office," *NK News*, March 31, 2015. *http://www.nknews.org/2015/03/n-korean-hacking-threat-leads-to-blue-house-cyber-security-office/.*

[36] Harper Neidig, "GOP Senator: North Korea Cyber Threat Growing," *The Hill*, October 7, 2015. *http://thehill.com/policy/cybersecurity/256274-gop-senator-north-korean-cyber-threat-growing.*

sistance to rogue states and non-state actors, would the DPRK also assist them with destructive cyber capabilities"?[37]

In addition, reports that the United States targeted the DPRK's nuclear program with a version of Stuxnet, but without success, may—if true—further complicate the challenge posed by North Korea.[38]

On many levels, North Korea is both a troubling and unusual case. Ordinarily, it is organized crime that seeks to penetrate the state. In this case, however, it is the other way around—with the state trying to penetrate organized crime in order to ensure the survival of the regime/dynasty.

Foreign Terrorist Organizations

To date, terrorist organizations have not demonstrated the advanced level of cyber attack capabilities that would be commensurate with these groups' stated ambitions. Undoubtedly, though, these organizations will persist in their efforts to augment their in-house cyber skills and capacities. Of particular concern are foreign terrorist organizations that benefit from state sponsorship and support, as well as the Islamic State in Iraq and Syria (ISIS/ISIL). Given ISIS' savvy use of social media and how it has built and maintained a sophisticated propaganda machine, it is likely that the group—and their sympathizers—will turn their efforts towards developing a more robust cyber attack capability.

The current level of cyber expertise possessed by terrorist groups should bring us little comfort, however, because a range of proxies for indigenous cyber capability exist: There is an arms bazaar of cyber weapons, and our adversaries need only intent and cash to access it. Capabilities, malware, weapons, etc.—all can be bought or rented.[39]

In terms of what we have seen recently, ISIS has invoked a new tactic against members of the U.S. military and law enforcement: "Doxing"—which involves gathering personal information from sources on-line and then publishing that data on-line, which puts the victim at risk of further attack in both the physical and virtual worlds.[40] A prevalent theme in the drumbeat of ISIS propaganda videos has been repeated calls for "lone wolf" attacks against Western law enforcement and military personnel.

Terrorist organizations also use the internet in a host of ways that serve to further their ends and put the United States and its allies, and the interests of both, in danger. By way of illustration, the internet helps terrorists plan and plot, radicalize and recruit, and train and fundraise. To help protect and facilitate these on-line activities, ISIS in particular has created "a new technical 'help desk'" that unifies its various tech support efforts, including for encryption.[41]

As terrorist cyber capabilities grow more sophisticated, one especially concerning scenario would involve terrorist targeting of U.S. critical infrastructure, using a mix of kinetic and cyber attacks. In this scenario, the cyber component could serve as a force multiplier to increase the lethality or impact of the physical attack.

Criminal Organizations

Cyber space has proven to be a gold mine for criminals, who have moved ever more deeply into the domain as opportunities to profit there continue to multiply. These criminal groups operate in layered organizations that share networks and tools. Despite reaping 30 cents on the dollar, there is a low chance that these criminals will be held accountable for their actions because they benefit from safe havens in Eastern Europe—which is, according to European Police Office (EUROPOL) Director Robert Wainwright, the source of 80 percent of all cyber crime.

The illicit activities of criminal groups in the virtual world are typically associated with the "Dark Web," a sub-set of the internet where the IP addresses of websites are concealed. Here, "the sale of drugs, weapons, counterfeit documents and child

---

[37] Rhea Siers, "North Korea: The Cyber Wild Card," Journal of Law & Cyber Warfare, 2014.

[38] Joseph Menn, "Exclusive: U.S. Tried Stuxnet-style Campaign Against North Korea but Failed—Sources," *Reuters*, May 29, 2015. *http://www.reuters.com/article/2015/05/29/us-usa-northkorea-stuxnet-idUSKBN0OE2DM20150529.*

[39] Frank Cilluffo, "Cyber Threats from China, Russia, and Iran: Protecting American Critical Infrastructure," Testimony before the U.S. House of Representatives, Committee on Homeland Security Subcommittee on Cybersecurity, Infrastructure Protection, and Security Technologies, March 20, 2013. *http://cchs.gwu.edu/sites/cchs.gwu.edu/files/downloads/Testimony_-Cilluffo_March_20_2013.pdf.*

[40] Kate Knibbs, "ISIS Has a New Terrorism Tactic: Doxing US Soldiers," *Gizmodo*, March 23, 2015. *http://gizmodo.com/isis-has-a-new-terrorism-tactic-doxing-us-soldiers-1693078782.*

[41] Cory Bennett, "New ISIS 'Help Desk' to Aid Hiding From Authorities," *The Hill*, February 10, 2016. *http://thehill.com/policy/cybersecurity/268940-new-isis-help-desk-unifies-encryption-support.*

pornography" constitute "vibrant industries."[42] Cyber criminals have also demonstrated substantial creativity, such as extortion schemes demanding payment via cryptocurrencies, such as Bitcoin. For example, most criminals demand payment for "ransomware" attacks (such as GameOver Zeus or CryptoLocker) to be made via cryptocurrencies, which are attractive to criminal organizations due to their anonymity or pseudonymity. Increasingly, more traditional organized crime groups, such as drug trafficking organizations, are also turning to virtual currencies for payment and to move their money in the black market.

According to EUROPOL whose focus is serious international organized crime, "cyber crime has been expanding to affect virtually all other criminal activities":

"The emergence of crime-as-a-service online has made cybercrime horizontal in nature, akin to activities such as money laundering or document fraud. The changing nature of cybercrime directly impacts on how other criminal activities, such as drug trafficking, the facilitation of illegal immigration, or the distribution of counterfeit goods are carried out . . . General trends for cybercrime suggest considerable increases in scope, sophistication, number and types of attacks, number of victims and economic damage . . . This allows traditional OCGs [organized criminal groups] to carry out more sophisticated crimes, buying access to the technical skills and expertise they require."[43]

Cyber criminals possess substantial cyber capabilities and, increasingly, are working with or for nation-states such as Russia. This convergence of forces heightens the dangers posed by both groups (e.g., criminal organizations and nation-states). And from a monetary standpoint alone, the amounts at stake are staggering. Consider: Russia's slice of the 2011 global cyber crime market has been pegged at $2.3 billion.[44]

"Hacktivists" and Other Entities

Cyber space largely levels the playing field, allowing individuals and small groups to have disproportionate impact. While some "hacktivists" may possess considerable abilities, the bar here is relatively low, and virtually anyone with a measure of skills and a special interest can cause harm.

Though great sophistication may not be needed to achieve disruption and draw attention to a particular concern, individuals and entities in this category can be a significant force, whether acting alone or loosely in tandem, essentially as a leaderless movement.

U.S. Response Measures

This varied threat landscape has a direct impact on a wide variety of cybersecurity policy questions facing the Congress and the Executive branch, including on current issues such as Federal spending on cybersecurity, the implementation of the new information-sharing law, Federal support for our critical infrastructure sectors, and the "going dark" debate over encryption in our electronic devices. In the remainder of my testimony, I will briefly highlight 2 important cyber issues that the GW Center for Cyber & Homeland Security is currently focusing on: Deterrence and active defense.

First, I will discuss deterrence. Having just racked and stacked the wide range of cyber threats that presently exist, and that may evolve and emerge in the future, the next step is to confront, contain, and thwart them by imposing significant costs on our adversaries for engaging in unacceptable behaviors.[45] Unless our adversaries experience such consequences, there will be little incentive for them to cease the actions and attacks in question. Changing their incentive structure requires signaling to hostile actors that the United States is both capable and willing to play offense. In turn, this means being more transparent about U.S. abilities and demonstrating the will to invoke them as required.

---

[42] Andy Greenberg, "Hacker Lexicon: What is the Dark Web?" *Wired*, November 19, 2014. *http://www.wired.com/2014/11/hacker-lexicon-whats-dark-web/*.

[43] "Massive Changes in the Criminal Landscape," Europol, 2015; and "Counterterrorism & Cybersecurity: Insights from Europol Director Rob Wainwright," *Center for Cyber and Homeland Security*, April 30, 2014. *https://www.europol.europa.eu/newsletter/massive-changes-criminal-landscape*; and *http://cchs.gwu.edu/counterterrorism-cybersecurity-insights-europol-director-rob-wainwright*.

[44] "Leading Russian Security Firm Group-IB Releases 2011 Report on Russian Cybercrime," *Group–IB*, April 24, 2012. *http://www.group-ib.com/?view=article&id=705*.

[45] Frank Cilluffo and Rhea Siers, "Cyber Deterrence is a Strategic Imperative," *The Wall Street Journal*, April 28, 2015; *http://blogs.wsj.com/cio/2015/04/28/cyber-deterrence-is-a-strategic-imperative/*; and *https://cchs.gwu.edu/sites/cchs.gwu.edu/files/downloads/INSS%20Blueprint%20for%20Cyber%20Deterrence.pdf*.

As things now stand however, our adversaries are acting largely without penalty and thus continue to transgress. Moreover when an incident occurs, our tendency is to blame the victim. This is a deeply flawed state of affairs that must be reversed. In fact, we should go further than simple reversal by working not only to deter our adversaries but to dissuade and compel them as well. Further elaborating U.S. policy and position in such a manner would be complementary to on-going U.S. and international efforts to enumerate and flesh out global norms of conduct for cyber space.

The second crucial shortcoming in current U.S. strategy and posture regards active defense, meaning the use of proactive measures by U.S. companies to defend themselves and their most critical assets against sophisticated and determined cyber adversaries. These adversaries include nation-states and their proxies. Although America's business community never asked to face off against foreign intelligence and security services (or those who would do their bidding), this is the position in which our companies find themselves. Accordingly, at minimum it is the responsibility of the U.S. Government to delineate and offer our private-sector partners an operating framework—that provides the parameters and supports that they need—in order to engage in active defense. The Center has formed a task force to examine these issues that is co-chaired by Admiral Dennis Blair, Secretary Michael Chertoff, Nuala O'Connor of the Center for Democracy & Technology, and me. We will be releasing a major report addressing these questions later this year.[46]

Concluding Thoughts

Looking ahead, many crucial questions on the threat side remain open, including: Will the nuclear weapons agreement concluded with Iran curb or embolden Iranian cyber operations against the United States and its allies over the longer term? Will the December 2015 cyber attack on Ukraine's electric grid, that caused a power outage in the western portion of the country, become a more commonplace tactic? Will hackers engage increasingly in data manipulation, as distinct from data theft? Equally important will be the attack vectors that, for whatever reason, we fail to anticipate. While we cannot know in advance every threat that may lurk around every virtual corner, we can certainly take the steps necessary to maximize our ability to detect, prevent, protect, and respond. In some instances, it may be that our ability to bounce back—our resilience—proves to be a valuable deterrent to our adversaries. At present however, there is still much work to be done before we can say that we have done all that we can. That work will be all the more crucial to accomplish as the Internet of Things expands exponentially the potential attack surface and leads the cyber domain to converge ever-further with the physical world. Secure design, architected from the get-go, will be crucial to resilience.[47]

Thank you again for this opportunity to testify on this important topic.[48] I look forward to trying to answer any questions that you may have.

Mr. RATCLIFFE. All right. Thank you, Mr. Cilluffo. The Chair now recognizes Ms. Kolde for 5 minutes for her opening statement.

STATEMENT OF JENNIFER KOLDE, LEAD TECHNICAL DIRECTOR, FIRE EYE THREAT INTELLIGENCE

Ms. KOLDE. Thank you, Mr. Chairman, Ranking Member Richmond, Congressman Marino, Congressman Donovan, thank you for the opportunity to speak with you today.

FireEye has a unique position within the security field. We have broad visibility across the threat landscape through a global network of over 10 million sensors. We have deep insight into threat actor activity through our Mandiant consulting and instant response practice, and we combine this visibility with contextual

[46] "Center Announces New Project on Active Defense against Cyber Threats," *GW Center for Cyber and Homeland Security*, February 4, 2016. *http://cchs.gwu.edu/center-announces-new-project-active-defense-against-cyber-threats.*

[47] Michael Papay, Frank Cilluffo, Sharon Cardash, "Opinion: Fortifying the Internet of Things means baking in security at the beginning," The Christian Science Monitor, March 6, 2015. *http://www.csmonitor.com/World/Passcode/Passcode-Voices/2015/0306/Opinion-Fortifying-the-Internet-of-Things-means-baking-in-security-at-the-beginning.*

[48] I would like to thank the Center's Associate Director Sharon Cardash for her help in drafting my prepared testimony.

analysis and intelligence through FireEye intelligence in our newly-acquired iSIGHT partners.

I have personally spent nearly 20 years in the information-sharing field in both the Government and private sector, including nearly 10 years using threat intelligence to identify and track sophisticated threat groups. I would like to describe the changing threat landscape as we see it.

FireEye currently tracks several hundred threat groups, including nation-state sponsor groups, cyber criminals, and terrorists. Across all of these groups, malicious activity continues to evolve more quickly than the ability of the private sector to safeguard assets, including financial data, personal health information, and intellectual property.

We continue to see operations from nation-state actors. This includes increased activities from countries such as Russia, whose actions have become both more public and more aggressive, as well as from Iran and North Korea, who while not as sophisticated have shown a willingness to engage in destructive attacks.

We also see operations from China-based groups, though it is premature to speculate whether or not this activity contravenes the recent agreements restricting commercial cyber espionage. At a minimum, we assess that China will continue to engage in cyber operations for the purpose of traditional espionage.

We also see cyber crime continue unabated. This includes well-known activity such as identity theft, financial fraud, and theft of payment card data.

However, cyber criminals are becoming more creative in their methods. Examples include hacking companies for insider business information in order to gain an advantage in the U.S. stock market and using extortion against corporations, whether that is ransomware used to encrypt corporate data or threatening to expose sensitive corporate information if the criminals are not paid.

We have directly observed very little activity that we would ascribe to cyber terrorists and their actions to date have largely been unsophisticated, such as defacements of websites and denial-of-service attacks. However, we assess that terrorist groups remain interested in cyber operations and recruiting individuals with advanced skills or insider access and could potentially carry out an impactful attack using only unsophisticated tools.

We also see an increase in the sophistication of the tools and techniques used by some of the nation-state and criminal groups that we monitor. This includes tools that can evade traditional operating system security and security software or that reside only in computer memory and leave very few forensic traces.

We also see increased efforts by the attackers to hide in plain sight so that hacker activity is indistinguishable from legitimate user behavior without using advanced detection methods.

These trends are concerning. Threat groups of all types continue to believe that cyber operations offer an asymmetric advantage. That is, groups with otherwise limited resources can obtain high rewards with low risk. Challenges inherent to our ability to effectively investigate, analyze, attribute, and prosecute activity leads to the sense that these groups can operate with impunity.

The challenges we face are many, and any solution to this complex problem must be multifaceted. I offer the following as essential, though not comprehensive, components to that solution.

First the public and private sectors must share information about malicious activity in a trusted, timely, and automated manner. However, the information shared cannot consist solely of technical indicators, but must be enhanced with contextual data that will allow defenders to prioritize alerts and respond faster and more effectively with appropriate countermeasures.

Second, we must understand that it is infeasible to secure networks or assets to prevent all possible attacks. Organizations must understand that real risks and advanced attacks will occur. We must proactively hunt for malicious activity that may have breached our defenses. We must be prepared to detect and respond to malicious activity across the entire attack life cycle.

Finally, we must continue to make it more difficult for attackers to reach their objectives. This should not be achieved by implementing compliance-type check lists, but through a risk-based approach where organizations identify critical assets and implement appropriate countermeasures based on a real-world understanding of how attackers operate.

By improving our defenses and the ability to quickly detect malicious activity, we may slow down attackers to give defenders more time to respond or, better yet, deter some opportunistic attackers all together.

Mr. Chairman, thank you for the opportunity, and I look forward to your questions.

[The prepared statement of Ms. Kolde follows:]

PREPARED STATEMENT OF JENNIFER KOLDE

FEBRUARY 25, 2016

Mr. Chairman, Ranking Member Richmond, and Members of the subcommittee, thank you for the opportunity to contribute to today's hearing. I am the lead technical director for threat intelligence at FireEye, a private company that provides software and services to detect and respond to digital intrusions. My testimony draws on our company's substantial experience remediating the most devastating breaches around the world by nation-state threat actors and cyber criminals and our advanced sensor network that protects our clients every day.

I have spent nearly 20 years in the information technology and information security fields, in roles from systems administration to network security to computer forensics and incident investigation. My experience includes 5 years as a computer scientist with the Federal Bureau of Investigation in support of cyber National security investigations. Following my Government service, I joined Mandiant—later acquired by FireEye—to help protect the private sector.

FireEye learns about the threat landscape through a unique combination of sources and methods:
- Our security consulting practice,
- Our global network of more than 10 million sensors, and
- A world-wide team of intelligence analysts.

Our consulting division, Mandiant, investigates and remediates the world's most devastating breaches; FireEye's endpoint and network sensors feed data to a repository of active cyber threat operations; and newly-acquired iSIGHT Partners offers unparalleled analytic insight. We use this robust set of data to correlate threat activity and characterize threat actors' capabilities and motivations. This combination of visibility and resources puts FireEye in a unique position to observe and analyze threat activity across a range of countries, industries, and customers, and to gain insight into adversarial operations during, after, and in some cases before an attack. I would like to describe the changing threat landscape as we see it.

THREAT ACTORS

I have spent nearly 10 years identifying and tracking sophisticated threat groups, both within the Government and the private sector. During that time I have watched the number of adversaries increase and their methods change dramatically. FireEye now tracks approximately 500 threat groups, including 29 advanced persistent threat (APT)[1] groups that we strongly suspect are supported by governments. Other tracked groups include criminals operating for financial gain, as well as others where we currently have insufficient information to characterize their activity.

This multitude of threat actors—suspected government actors and enterprise cyber criminals alike—continues to evolve more quickly than the ability of the private sector to safeguard assets, including financial data, personal health information, and intellectual property.

Governments

FireEye has regularly observed cyber threat activity from individuals we believe are sponsored by government agencies. While China has always been a prominent player in this area, in recent years we have seen additional threats from countries including Russia, Iran, North Korea, and Syria. This is likely due both to increased visibility into these threats, as well as an actual uptick in activity as nations attempt to increase and refine their capabilities in the cyber realm.

China

China-based groups have historically been the most prolific threat actors we observed in terms of the number of distinct threat groups and the number of victim organizations. The agreement reached in September between Chinese President Xi Jinping and President Barack Obama to restrict commercial cyber espionage has the potential to significantly realign the threat landscape. FireEye continues to monitor known and suspected activity from China-based groups, but we believe it is still too early to draw definitive conclusions about China's compliance or lack thereof with the agreement and how or whether China may change its operations. At a minimum, we assess that China will continue to engage in cyber espionage against the United States to obtain political and foreign policy information, to gain insight into the U.S. activities of activists and religious and ethnic minorities advocating change in China, and possibly to acquire security-related information from private companies with a clear tie to national defense.

Russia

Russia has become increasingly aggressive over the past few years, both geopolitically and in cyber space. Russia has always held a reputation as a skilled and stealthy cyber opponent, but recently their activities have been more widely exposed and discussed, including by FireEye in our reporting on groups we call APT28 and APT29. Despite on-going publicity surrounding their tools and operations, we have seen no significant drop in their activity. APT28 has used zero-day exploits and spear phishing to aggressively pursue military and political secrets in the United States, Europe, the Middle East, and the Asia-Pacific region. APT29, which we have observed through incident response engagements, proved to be a skilled and adaptable opponent. Many groups will go silent or abandon victim networks when discovered. However, in this case APT29 battled to retain control of the environment using speed and scale that would outmatch all but the most skilled and advanced network defenders.

Russia also appears to use its cyber skills in support of real-world military or information warfare operations. Examples include suspicions that Russian state-sponsored hackers were behind December 2015 power outages in the Ukraine, as well as a suspected "false flag" operation by APT28: While purportedly a pro-Jihadist activist group calling themselves the "CyberCaliphate" was responsible for an attack on French media outlet TV5Monde in April 2015, technical indicators suggest that APT28 was actually responsible.

Iran and North Korea

Iran and North Korea are more recent players on the stage, though what they currently lack in capability and sophistication they have been willing to make up for in brazenness. Both have demonstrated the intent and willingness to employ disruptive operations through denial of service or destructive malware—Iran purport-

---

[1] Advanced Persistent Threat (APT) actors are assessed to take direction from a nation-state to steal information or conduct network attacks, tenaciously pursue their objectives, and are capable of using a range of tools and tactics.

edly overwriting data on thousands of computers at Saudi Aramco in 2012, and North Korea in a similar attack on Sony Pictures Entertainment in 2014.

To date, neither Iran nor North Korea has matched the scope of operations or level of sophistication seen by countries such as China or Russia. Iran is believed to have targeted U.S. defense companies, politicians, and policy makers, as well as political dissidents and reporters or members of the media. These types of attacks were documented in FireEye's report on "Operation Saffron Rose" and in the iSIGHT Partners—now part of FireEye—report on the "Newscaster" activity.

Both Iran and North Korea have been successful despite relative isolation from the global computer security community. Iranian attackers have custom tools including some made by domestic security companies, but they also use publicly-available tools. Iranian threat groups frequently rely on spear phishing and social engineering techniques to trick victims into installing malware or providing usernames and passwords to fake login sites, as opposed to leveraging exploits to compromise computers.

Interestingly, as Iran and North Korea attempt to increase their capabilities in the cyber realm, they appear to be taking lessons not only in tools and techniques, but also in stealth and "false flag" operations. Iran has frequently leveraged social media, creating fake profiles used to connect with targets to learn about victims' movements, activities, and other connections. Several operations believed to have been carried out by North Korea were executed to appear to be the responsibility of hacktivists or patriotic hackers.

Cyber Criminals

Cyber crime continues to be a concern, impacting individual citizens through identity theft and corporations through large-scale financial fraud and associated costs, including network remediation and reissuance of payment cards. Theft of payment card data continues unabated, with merchants of all sizes affected. However, as the value of payment card and bank account data decreases in the criminal underground, cyber criminals are becoming more innovative in their methods to steal and monetize organizations' information. For example, FireEye identified criminal activity in 2014, carried out by a group we call FIN4, where that group stole insider information from pharmaceutical, health care, and consulting companies to gain a competitive advantage in capital markets in the United States.

We are also seeing a rise in the use of ransomware-malware that encrypts the victim's data, requiring them to pay a ransom to the cyber criminal to "unlock" or decrypt their information. Criminals originally used ransomware targeted at individual computers to charge small unlocking fees, but we are now seeing criminals target organizations with more sizeable extortion demands to restore encrypted corporate data. These types of attacks could have significant impact if carried out against organizations that provide essential services or support critical infrastructure, including agencies and departments in the U.S. Government.

Beyond ransomware, criminals may take a cue from recent nation-state activity, and conduct extortion not merely by encrypting data, but by threatening to destroy computers or expose sensitive company data. The Sony Pictures incident, where both techniques were used, played out very publicly and very effectively for the attackers. Given law enforcement's limited ability to identify and prosecute perpetrators outside their borders or otherwise impose meaningful consequences, criminals may be emboldened to raise the stakes in exchange for a higher ransom.

Terrorists

To date, FireEye has observed very little cyber activity that we would directly attribute to terrorist groups. Most of the cyber activity from groups claiming affiliation with terrorist organizations, including groups claiming affiliation with the Islamic State, has been unsophisticated. Our company does not monitor terrorist social media use, but we assess these groups are using social networks to recruit individuals with advanced cyber skills. Other potential recruitment targets would include insiders who could facilitate cyber operations, based on the behavior of cyber crime groups who assemble their teams this way.

Terrorists are likely to continue using cyber operations to target and expose seemingly sensitive data, such as lists of Government and military employees, most of which is gained through careful collection of publicly-available information or by targeting personal accounts. We believe that most terrorist organizations currently do not have the capability to carry out sophisticated cyber attacks on their own, and would need to cultivate those capabilities through recruitment of highly-skilled individuals, or through sufficient funds to purchase or hire such expertise. Current capabilities are likely limited to blunt attacks such as denial-of-service or destruction of data or resources, possibly carried out in concert with a kinetic attack.

INFORMATION SHARING

Information sharing is critical to the ability of the United States to successfully defend itself in cyber space. It will not, however, eliminate the risk of cyber attacks.

To defeat the most advanced threat groups, the private and public sector must share information not only about technical indicators—which are reactive—but about motivations, plans, and intentions that would enable forewarning. This information must be Unclassified and shared in near-real-time for network defenders to regain the upper hand against the best state-sponsored threat groups. Information sharing must be part of a comprehensive security strategy and combined with broader efforts to educate organizations about real risks, train security personnel to combat them effectively, and develop incentives so that the public and private sectors are motivated to invest in protecting data, assets, and critical infrastructure.

REWARD OUTWEIGHS RISK

I have described how threat actors have increased in number and sophistication, and how groups of all types who once had only limited cyber capabilities have become more of a threat. This trend is due to multiple factors, including:
- The asymmetric advantage of cyber operations. Groups with otherwise limited military, political, or economic capabilities can leverage cyber operations to damage an opponent or deliver a political message, often with limited investment in resources and to disproportionate effect.
- The on-going perception that threat groups can largely operate with impunity. The rewards to be had from conducting cyber operations greatly outweigh the risks, for state-sponsored, criminal, and terrorist hacking groups alike.

The perception of low risk and high reward for nation-state, criminal, and terrorist groups alike stems from a number of challenges related to the investigation, analysis, attribution, and prosecution of activity in the cyber realm:
- Forensic data can be volatile in the best of circumstances, and many groups take pains to limit or delete traces of their activity, further undermining investigators' ability to understand what occurred.
- Cyber crime and cyber operations are not limited by geographical boundaries, and groups may deliberately spread their activity across multiple countries to mislead and complicate investigation and prosecution.
- The ability to discern a threat group's true purpose and motivation becomes more difficult as nation-state and criminal actors adopt each other's tools and techniques. Groups may also attempt to actively misdirect investigators using "false flag" efforts.
- Attribution—the ability to link activity in the cyber realm to a real-world person or group—remains challenging, whether attempting to identify a criminal or a foreign government.

The challenges we face in the current threat landscape are many, but they are not insurmountable. Complex problems require multi-faceted solutions. I offer the following suggestions to facilitate these efforts:
- Continue to facilitate safe, trusted, and automated means for the public and private sector to share information about current and emerging threats. This sharing should encompass not merely indicators, but also contextual data about the nature, scope, and risk associated with those indicators. Context enables prioritization and decision making, allowing defenders to respond faster and more effectively.
- Recognize that the "fortress" approach of attempting to fully secure our networks and assets to prevent all possible attacks is infeasible. Organizations must secure their environments to the best of their ability, but understand that breaches can and will occur, and that they must have tools and resources in place to detect, respond to, and contain malicious activity across the entire attack life cycle.
- Identify ways that organizations can "raise the bar" attackers must overcome to achieve their objectives. While the complexities of investigation and attribution may make it difficult to impact threat actors in the wake of an attack, we can work together to make attacks more difficult and costly to carry out. This process may deter opportunistic attackers and slow down determined threats, giving defenders more time to detect and respond to attacks.

Mr. Chairman, Ranking Member Richmond, and Members of the subcommittee, I thank you for your attention and time today. I look forward to answering your questions.

Mr. RATCLIFFE. Thank you. The Chair now recognizes Mr. Bromwich for 5 minutes.

STATEMENT OF ADAM BROMWICH, VICE PRESIDENT, SECU-RITY TECHNOLOGY AND RESPONSE, SYMANTEC, TESTI-FYING ON BEHALF OF THE CYBER THREAT ALLIANCE

Mr. BROMWICH. Chairman Ratcliffe, Ranking Member Richmond, and Members of the committee, thank you for the opportunity to testimony today. Your focus on emerging threats is right on point, because more than perhaps any other security discipline, cybersecurity is constantly evolving.

Many of the recent headlines about cyber attacks have highlighted data breaches in Government and across the spectrum of industries, but cyber attacks encompass more than just breaches. The incidents we see today raise from basic confidence schemes to sophisticated and potentially destructive intrusions into critical infrastructure systems.

The attackers run the gamut and include highly-organized criminal enterprises, disgruntled employees, individual cyber criminals, so-called hacktivists, and state-sponsored groups. Common attack types range from distributed denial-of-service, or DDOS, to highly-targeted attacks, to widely-distributed financial fraud scams.

A DDOS attack is an attempt to overwhelm a system with data, while targeted attacks typically try to trick someone into opening an infected file or clicking on a bad link. Of course, scams and blackmail schemes for profit continue.

One of the most common is ransomware, which locks the victim's computer and displays a screen that purports to be from law enforcement. The attackers demand payment of a fine for having illegal content on the computer. But criminals are always looking for new ways to make money. They have moved beyond ransomware and are now frequently using a more insidious and harmful form of malware known as crypto lockers. While most scams are classic confidence schemes, ransom script is straight-up blackmail. Pay a ransom or your computer files will be lost.

The criminals use high-grade encryption technology to scramble the victim's computer, and only the attacker has the key to unlock it. In the past month, Hollywood Presbyterian Hospital in California fell victim to just this kind of attack. Over a 10-day period, staff was forced to use pen and paper until the hospital paid the criminals a $17,000 ransom for the decryption key needed to unlock their computers. Some medical devices were reportedly off-line. Wait times increased at the emergency room. Some patients were directed to other hospitals.

The attacker surface is always shifting, and the enormous growth of connected devices, commonly referred to as the Internet of Things, or IOT, will bring with it a new generation of attacks. Last summer, the remote compromise of a Jeep automobile by a pair of security researchers received a great deal of attention. Receiving less attention, but equally concerning are several alerts about vulnerabilities in drug and fusion pumps that the Department of Homeland Security issued over the past year. If a device is running software and it is connected to the internet, vulnerabilities can enable attackers to take control.

Attack methods are always evolving and improving. The most common attack method, spearfishing, uses customized, targeted e-mails containing malware or malicious links. Social media is an increasingly valuable tool for attackers, as people tend to trust links in postings that appear to come from a friend's social media feed. We have also seen the rapid growth of targeted, web-based attacks known as watering hole attacks.

These techniques, while originally used only by sophisticated and well-resourced attackers, are now available as tool kits that can any criminal can purchase and use. Attacks are getting more sophisticated, but so, too, are security tools. Most attacks, including recent high-profile breaches, could have been prevented if organizations implemented the latest cybersecurity technology and best practices.

To block advanced threats and zero-day attacks, intelligence machine learning and advanced exploit prevention technologies are necessary. These tools use automation to train a system to identify an attack, even one that has never been seen before. It is also increasingly critical to use big data analytics to evaluate global software patterns. At Symantec, these analytics are able to identify and block entirely new attacks purely by evaluating relationships with other devices and other files across a global network of hundreds of millions of computers.

Cooperation is also key to improving cybersecurity, and we participate in numerous industry consortia and public-private partnerships to combat cyber crime. These include the National Cyber Forensics and Training Alliance, or NCFTA, the FBI, Europol, Interpol, the North Atlantic Treaty Organization, and Ameripol. We have also been involved in numerous operations to take down criminal networks, including the operations that took down the ransomware network CryptoLocker, the Dridex financial fraud botnet, and the Ramnit botnet.

Just yesterday, Symantec participated in a collaborative cross-industry operation that targeted an aggressive threat group known as Lazarus. This is the same group thought to be behind the Sony attack. The initiative called Operation Blockbuster significantly bolstered defenses against the cyber espionage group and it is disruptive campaigns.

Cooperation within the security industry is important, and in 2014, Symantec, Palo Alto Networks, Fortinet and Intel Security formed the Cyber Threat Alliance to better distribute detailed information about advanced attacks. CTA shares high-value, actionable threat intelligence while still maintaining the privacy and confidentiality of all customer data.

The partnership works because it is not about one vendor trying to gain advantage. We are all contributing and sharing with the community to better uncover, understand, and protect against advanced attacks. The cyber threat landscape is always evolving, but so, too, are new security technologies. Preventing cyber crime is a shared effort, and your work to inform the public is an important part of that.

We appreciate the opportunity to testify today, and I am happy to take any questions you have.

[The prepared statement of Mr. Bromwich follows:]

PREPARED STATEMENT OF ADAM BROMWICH

FEBRUARY 25, 2016

Chairman Ratcliffe, Ranking Member Richmond, and Members of the committee, my name is Adam Bromwich and I am the vice president of Symantec's Security Technology and Response (STAR) team. I lead a global team of engineers, researchers, and analysts who develop our security technologies, attack intelligence, and security content. My team is on the front lines of cybersecurity, identifying the latest attack patterns and campaigns, deploying protection to our customers around the clock from research centers across the globe, and working closely with law enforcement agencies to track cyber criminal groups. Prior to this role, I led the development and launch of our Insight reputation technology, a fundamentally new protection approach that leverages big data analytics and anonymous software adoption patterns from over 50 million endpoints to automatically compute safety ratings for virtually every software file and web site on the internet. I also served as director of advanced concepts, an incubator group within Symantec Research Labs, where I developed new products including the Norton Online Family child safety software. I received my Bachelor of Arts degree from Princeton University and an MBA from Yale University.

Symantec protects much of the world's information, and is the largest security software company in the world with 33 years of experience developing cybersecurity technology and helping consumers, businesses, and governments secure and manage their information and identities. Our products and services protect people's information and their privacy across platforms—from the smallest mobile device, to the enterprise data center, to cloud-based systems. We have established some of the most comprehensive sources of cyber threat data in the world through our Global Intelligence Network, which is comprised of hundreds of millions of attack sensors recording hundreds of thousands of events per second, and more than 1,000 dedicated security engineers and analysts. We maintain 9 Security Response Centers and 6 Security Operations Centers around the globe. Every day we scan 30 percent of the world's enterprise email traffic, and process more than 1.8 billion web requests. All of these resources combined allow us to capture world-wide security data that give our analysts a unique view of the entire cyber threat landscape.

The title of today's hearing is instructive, and I am glad to see a focus on "emerging" threats. More than perhaps any other security discipline, cybersecurity is not static. Attackers are always innovating and threats evolve quickly. Just the same, defenses cannot be static. In my testimony today, I will discuss:

- The current and emerging threat environment;
- Cutting-edge technologies to counter the latest threats;
- How we work with the Government to improve cybersecurity and stop criminals; and
- How we partner with our industry colleagues to counter cyber attacks.

I. THE CURRENT CYBER THREAT LANDSCAPE

Many of the recent headlines about cyber attacks have focused on data breaches in Government and across the spectrum of industries. Indeed, the volume of recent thefts of personally identifiable information (PII) is unprecedented—over just the past 3 years alone, the number of identities exposed through breaches surpassed 1 billion. Yet while the focus on data breaches and the identities put at risk is certainly warranted, we also must not lose sight of the other types of cyber attacks that are equally concerning and can have damaging consequences. There are a wide set of tools available to the cyber attacker, and the incidents we see today range from basic confidence schemes to massive denial-of-service attacks to sophisticated (and potentially destructive) intrusions into critical infrastructure systems. The economic impact can be immediate with the theft of money, or more long-term and structural, such as through the theft of intellectual property. It can ruin a company or individual's reputation or finances, and it can impact citizens' trust in the internet and their Government.

While many assume that breaches are the result of sophisticated malware or a well-resourced state actor, the reality is much more troubling. According to a 2015 report from the Online Trust Alliance, 90 percent of recent breaches could have been prevented if organizations implemented basic cybersecurity best practices.[1] More-

---

[1] https://www.otalliance.org/news-events/press-releases/ota-determines-over-90-data-breaches-2014-could-have-been-prevented.

over, some breaches are actually second-generation activity—criminals leverage previously stolen personal information to compromise an individual's account.

The attackers run the gamut and include highly-organized criminal enterprises, disgruntled employees, individual cybercriminals, so-called "hacktivists," and state-sponsored groups. The motivations vary—the criminals generally are looking for some type of financial gain, the hacktivists are seeking to promote or advance some cause, and the state actors can be engaged in espionage (traditional spycraft or economic) or infiltrating critical infrastructure systems. These lines, however, are not set in stone, as criminals and even state actors might pose as hacktivists, and criminals often offer their skills to the highest bidder. Attribution has always been difficult in cyber space, and is further complicated by the ability of cyber actors to mask their motives and objectives through misdirection and obfuscation.

Common Types of Attacks

Distributed Denial-of-Service ("DDoS")

Distributed denial-of-service (DDoS) attacks attempt to deny service to legitimate users by overwhelming the target with activity. The most common method is to flood a server with network traffic from multiple sources (hence "distributed"). These attacks are often conducted through "botnets"—armies of compromised computers that are made up of victim machines that stretch across the globe and are controlled by "bot herders" or "bot masters."[2]

DDoS attacks have grown larger year over year, from the equivalent of a garden hose to a fire hose to the outflow pipes of the Hoover dam. Even the most prepared networks can buckle under that volume of data the first time it is directed at them, which is why a few years ago even some of the Nation's biggest financial institutions initially suffered outages when they were victims of a DDoS campaign. In addition to increasing in volume, the attacks are getting more sophisticated and vary the methods used, which makes them harder to mitigate.

The purpose of most attacks is to disrupt, not to destroy. However, some sophisticated attackers will use a DDoS attack to distract an organization's security team while the criminals unleash a more sophisticated attack. For instance, organized crime groups have been known to initiate DDoS attacks against banks to divert the attention and resources of the bank's security team while the main attack is launched, which can include draining customer accounts or stealing credit card information.

Targeted Attacks

Targeted attacks are increasingly common. Some are directed at a company's servers and systems, where attackers search for unpatched vulnerabilities on websites or undefended connections to the internet. But many rely on social engineering, conning people into clicking on a link, opening a file, or taking some other action that will allow an attacker to compromise their device. The attack can be targeted at almost any level, even at an entire sector of the economy or a group of similar organizations or companies. Attacks also can target a particular company or a unit within a company (e.g., research and development or finance) or even a specific person.

Most of the data breaches and other attacks that have been in the news were the result of a targeted attack, but the goal of the attacker can vary greatly. One constant is that after attackers select a target they will set out to gain access to the systems they want to compromise and once inside there are few limits on what they can do if the target is not well-protected. The malware used today is largely commoditized, and while we still see some that is custom-crafted, most of the attacks rely on attack kits that are sold on the cyber black market. But even these commodity attack kits are highly sophisticated and are designed to avoid detection—some even come with guarantees from the criminal seller that they will not be stopped by common security measures. This makes it all the more important—but also more challenging—to stay ahead of the attackers.

Scams, Blackmail, and Other Cyber Theft

Like most crime, cyber attacks are often financially motivated, and some of the most common (and most successful) involve getting victims to pay out money, whether through trickery or direct threats. One early and widely successful attack of this type was known as "scareware." Scareware is a form of malware that will open a window on your device that claims your system is infected, and offer to "clean" it for a fee. Some forms of scareware open pop-ups falsely claiming to be from major security companies (including Symantec), and if a user clicks on the win-

---

[2] "Bots and Botnets—A Growing Threat," *Symantec*, *http://us.norton.com/botnet/*.

dow they are taken to a fake website that can look very much like that of the real company. Of course, in most cases the only infection on your computer is the scareware itself. Victims who fall for the scam are lucky if they only lose the $20 or $30 "cost" for the fake software, but most are out much more as they typically provide credit card information to pay the scammer in the mistaken belief they are purchasing legitimate security software. Not only did they authorize a payment to the scammer, but they also provided financial information that could then be sold on the criminal underground. And by allowing the scammer to install the supposed cleaning software on their device, they give the criminal the ability to install additional malware and potentially steal more financial information or turn their system into a zombie soldier in a botnet.

First widely seen in 2007, scareware began to diminish in 2011 after users became alerted to the scams and they became much less effective. Criminals next turned to "ransomware," which has grown significantly since 2012. Ransomware is another type of deception where the malware locks the victim's device and displays a screen that purports to be from a law enforcement entity local to the user. The lock screen states that there is illegal content on the computer—everything from pirated movies to child pornography—and instructs the victim to pay a "fine" for their "crime." The criminals claim that the victim's device will be unlocked once the "fine" is paid, but in reality the device frequently remains locked. Both of these types of attacks can be removed from your computer and we offer instructions and free tools on our *Norton.com* website to assist victims in doing so.

Criminals have now moved beyond even ransomware and are using a more insidious and harmful form of malware known as "ransomcrypt." While scareware and ransomware are more classic confidence schemes, ransomcrypt is straight-up blackmail: Pay a ransom or your computer files will be erased. And unlike scareware and ransomware, there is often no way to get rid of it—the criminals use high-grade encryption technology to scramble the victim's computer, and only they have the key to unlock it. Unless the system is backed up, the victim faces the difficult choice of paying the criminals or losing all the data. Last year one police department in Maine paid a ransom in order to regain control of its data.[3] The police chief said "[w]e needed our programs to get back on-line."[4] A more recent example is the compromise of the systems at Hollywood Presbyterian Hospital. Over a 10-day period, staff was forced to use pen and paper until the hospital paid the criminals a $17,000 ransom for the decryption key needed to unlock their computers. Some medical devices were reportedly off-line, wait times increased at the emergency room, and some patients were directed to other hospitals.

Emerging Threats

Attackers are constantly looking for new devices to compromise and new vectors to use to attack them, and the enormous growth of connected devices, commonly referred to as the Internet of Things or IoT, is significantly expanding the available attack surface. Last summer the remote compromise of a Jeep by a pair of security researchers received a great deal of attention, and with good reason.[5] The video of the reporter driving on the highway while unable to control the car as traffic rushed past was frightening and powerful. Receiving less attention, but equally concerning, are several alerts about vulnerabilities in drug infusion pumps that the Department of Homeland Security's Industrial Control System Computer Emergency Response Team issued over the past year.[6]

These are just 2 examples of vulnerabilities in connected devices, and how the explosive growth of such connections can lead to physical harm. The potential for scams and other financial fraud is just as great. We need to be prepared for ransomware targeted at a smartwatch—or a connected thermostat, refrigerator, or automobile. Criminals know that most consumers would pay a few hundred dollars in blackmail to regain control of a $50,000 vehicle that was rendered unusable by a piece of targeted malware.

Yet while the devices that could be compromised are new, many of the underlying reasons they are susceptible to attack are not. In fact, many of the new connected devices are not being built with security as a core design principle, and too many of the deployed devices are not protected or updated. Last year we released a report

[3] Stephanie Mlot, "Maine Police Pay Ransomware Demand in Bitcoin," *PCmag*, April 14, 2015, *http://www.pcmag.com/article2/0,2817,2481356,00.asp*.
[4] Id.
[5] Andy Greenberg, "Hackers Remotely Kill a Jeep on the Highway—With Me in It," *Wired*, July 21, 2015, *http://www.wired.com/2015/07/hackers-remotely-kill-jeep-highway/*.
[6] See, e.g., *https://ics-cert.us-cert.gov/advisories/ICSA-15-337-02* (January 21, 2016); *https://ics-cert.us-cert.gov/advisories/ICSA-15-125-01B* (June 10, 2015).

titled "Insecurity in the Internet of Things"[7] that analyzed 50 "smart home" devices. The findings were shocking: Among other security issues, none of the devices enforced strong passwords, followed appropriate authentication protocols, or protected accounts against brute-force attacks. Almost 20 percent of the mobile apps used to control the tested IoT devices did not encrypt communications to the cloud—which means they were transmitting data in clear text across the internet.

All of these potential weaknesses are already well-known to the security industry, yet known mitigation techniques are often neglected on these devices. These findings were consistent with those of a previous report we issued in 2014, which examined security in health and fitness tracking devices, many of which transmitted data (including passwords) in clear text and failed to conduct proper authentication before connecting with outside devices or systems.[8] These devices can be protected, and they can be built with that in mind, but that needs to start at the design stage to lay the groundwork for strong security over the life of the device.

Another worrisome trend is the increase in destructive malware such as the one used against Sony in 2014. In the past attackers were focused on stealing data, holding it ransom, or conducting espionage. But the Sony malware did much more—it completely erased hard drives and rendered computers unusable.[9] While still the minority of attacks, we expect to see more of them in the future. This only further highlights the need for organizations to be proactive about security and to utilize modern tools to protect their systems and contain any intrusion.

Methods Attackers Use to Compromise Systems

All of the attacks outlined above started with a common factor—a compromised device. From this one device, attackers often are able to move within a system until they achieve their ultimate goal. But the threshold question is how do they get that foothold—how do they make that initial compromise that allows them to infiltrate a system?

We frequently hear about the sophistication of various attackers and about "Advance Persistent Threats" or "APTs," but the discussion of cyber attacks—and of cyber defense—often ignores the psychology leading up to the exploit. Most attacks rely on social engineering—in the simplest of terms, trying to trick people into doing something that they would never do if fully cognizant of their actions. For this reason, we often say that the most successful attacks are as much psychology as they are technology.

Spear phishing, or customized, targeted emails containing malware, is the most common form of attack. Attackers harvest publicly-available information and use it to craft an email designed to dupe a specific victim or group of victims. The goal is to get victims to open a document or click on a link to a website that will then try to infect their computers. While good security will stop most of these attacks—which often seek to exploit older, known vulnerabilities—many organizations and individuals do not have up-to-date security or properly patched operating systems or software. And many of these attacks are extremely well-crafted; in the case of one major attack, the spear phishing email was so convincing that even though the victim's system automatically routed it to junk mail, he retrieved it and opened it—and exposed his company to a major breach.

Social media is an increasingly valuable tool for cyber criminals in two different ways. First, it is particularly effective in direct attacks, as people tend to trust links and postings that come from a friend's social media feed (or appear to) and rarely stop to question if that feed may have been compromised or spoofed. Thus, attackers target social media accounts and then use them to "like" or otherwise promote a posting that contains a malicious link. Social media is also widely used to conduct reconnaissance for spear phishing or other highly-targeted attacks as it often provides just the kind of personal details that a skilled attacker can use to get a victim to let his or her guard down.

Beginning in 2012, we saw the rapid growth of a new type of targeted web-based attack, known as a "watering hole" attack. Like the lion in the wild who stalks a watering hole for unsuspecting prey, cyber criminals have become adept at lying in wait on legitimate websites and using them to try to infect visitors' computers. They do so by compromising legitimate websites that their victims are likely to visit and modifying them so that they will surreptitiously try to infect visitors or redirect

---

[7] *https://www.symantec.com/content/dam/symantec/docs/white-papers/insecurity-in-the-internet-of-things.pdf.*

[8] *https://www.symantec.com/content/dam/symantec/docs/white-papers/how-safe-is-your-quantified-self.pdf.*

[9] Sean Gallagher, "Inside the 'wiper' malware that brought Sony Pictures to its knees," *Ars Technica*, December 3, 2014, *http://arstechnica.com/security/2014/12/inside-the-wiper-malware-that-brought-sony-pictures-to-its-knees/.*

them to a malicious site. For example, one attacker targeted mobile application developers by compromising a site that was popular with them. In another case, we saw employees from 500 different companies in the same industry visit one compromised site in just 24 hours, each running the risk of infection.[10] Cyber criminals gained control of these websites through many of the same tactics described above—spear phishing and other social engineering attacks on the site managers, developers, or owners. Many of these websites were compromised through known attack vectors, meaning that good security practices could have prevented them from being compromised.

II. MODERN SECURITY TOOLS

Attacks are getting more sophisticated, but so too are security tools. Security still starts with basic measures such as strong passwords or multi-factor authentication and up-to-date patch management. But while these steps may stop many older, simpler attacks, they will be little more than a speed bump for even a moderately sophisticated attacker.

Real protection requires a modern security suite that is being fully utilized. To block advanced threats and zero-day attacks, sophisticated machine learning and advanced exploit prevention technologies are necessary. These approaches are able to use automation to train a system to identify an attack, even one that has never been seen before. It is also increasingly critical to use big data analytics to evaluate global software patterns to create real-time intelligence. Today these analytics are able to identify and block entirely new attacks by evaluating how they are distributed and their relationships with other devices and other files.

Data protection is equally important, and a comprehensive security program includes data loss prevention (DLP) tools that index, track, and control the access to and movement of huge volumes of data across an organization. Perhaps most importantly, DLP tools will prevent that data from moving outside an organization. Organizations should also use encryption technology on particularly sensitive data, which renders it unreadable to anyone who does not have the specific cryptologic key.

Device-specific protections are also important. For example, in the retail world, there are tools that can be applied to point-of-sale systems that will virtually lock down the system and only allow it to perform those limited functions that are absolutely necessary for completing a sales transaction. In the IoT world, there are authentication, encryption, and end-point protection tools that are designed to run on small and low-power devices. These tools can protect everything from a connected vehicle to the small sensors built into a bridge or that monitor critical machinery.

In short, good security does not happen by accident—it requires planning and continued attention. But criminals will always be evolving, and security must as well.

III. PUBLIC-PRIVATE PARTNERSHIPS TO ENHANCE CYBERSECURITY

Every day we hear about the impact of cyber crime, but we do not often hear about the many successes that law enforcement and the private sector have had in stopping these crimes and bringing these criminals to justice. Recently, we have seen a string of successful arrests and prosecutions of some of the most notorious cyber criminals in the world. In July 2015, a New York judge sentenced Alexander Yucel, the creator of the "Black Shades" Trojan to 5 years in prison and the forfeiture of $200,000. Yucel was swept up by the Federal Bureau of Investigation (FBI) and Europol last year along with dozens of other individuals in the United States and abroad. Symantec worked closely with the FBI in this coordinated takedown effort, sharing information that allowed the agency to track down those suspected of involvement. And in June 2015, Ercan "Segate" Findikoglu, the man who prosecutors say orchestrated one of the biggest cyber bank heists in American history was extradited to the United States to stand trial for stealing more than $55 million by hacking bank computers and withdrawing millions in cash from ATMs.

In fact, over the last few years we have had a number of successful takedown operations against prominent financial fraud botnets. In June of 2014, the FBI, the United Kingdom (UK) National Crime Agency, and a number of international law enforcement agencies mounted a major operation against the financial fraud botnet Gameover Zeus and the ransomware network Cryptolocker. Gameover Zeus was the largest financial fraud botnet in operation in 2014 and is often described as one of the most technically sophisticated variants of the ubiquitous Zeus malware. Symantec provided technical insights into the operation and impact of both Gameover Zeus and Cryptolocker, and worked with a broad industry coalition and

---

[10] Symantec, "Internet Security Threat Report, Volume XVIII," April 16, 2013, Pg. 21.

the FBI during this case. As a result, authorities were able to seize a large portion of the infrastructure used by the cyber criminals behind both threats.

And in February of 2015, a Europol-led operation struck against the Ramnit botnet and seized its servers and infrastructure. Ramnit facilitated a vast cyber crime operation, harvesting banking credentials and other personal credentials from its victims. The group was in operation for at least 5 years and in that time evolved into a major criminal operation, infecting more than 3.2 million computers. These law enforcement operations and others have knocked out or severely curtailed the operations of some of the most prominent financial fraud groups in the world. In fact, the number of bots declined by 18 percent in 2014 compared to the previous year. In large measure, this decline is because the FBI, the Europol European Cybercrime Centre (EC3), and other international law enforcement agencies, working with Symantec and other technology companies, disrupted and shut them down.

Because cyber space is a domain without borders, where crimes are often committed at a great distance, every device in the United States is a potential border entry point, making investigation and prosecution of cyber crimes a difficult task. This reality makes international engagement on cybersecurity essential. For example, Symantec partnered with AMERIPOL and the Organization of American States to publish a report that provides the most comprehensive snapshot to date of cybersecurity threats in the Latin America and Caribbean region. The goal was to raise awareness of cyber crime issues and promote the importance of cybersecurity throughout the region as a National and economic security imperative.

Similarly, Symantec is partnering with the African Union to develop a report looking at the cybersecurity threats and trends in Africa. That report will be published later this year.

Symantec also maintains relationships in the United States and around the world with international cyber response organizations and law enforcement entities including INTERPOL, EUROPOL, and dozens of National Computer Emergency Response Teams (CERTs) and police forces, by sharing the latest technological trends, the evolution of the threat landscape, and the techniques that cyber criminals use to launch attacks. Our latest partnership, signed in December 2015, is with the North Atlantic Treaty Organization (NATO), and is focused on boosting 2-way threat information sharing.

IV. PRIVATE-SECTOR PARTNERSHIPS TO ENHANCE CYBERSECURITY—THE CYBER THREAT ALLIANCE

In 2014, Symantec, Fortinet, Intel Security, and Palo Alto Networks formed the Cyber Threat Alliance (CTA) to work together to share threat information. The goal was to better distribute detailed information about advanced attacks and thereby raise the situational awareness of CTA members and improve overall protection for our customers. Since the founding of the CTA, several contributing members have joined, including Barracuda Networks, Reversing Labs, Zscaler, and ElevenPaths (part of Telefonica). Prior industry sharing efforts were often limited to the exchange of malware samples, and the CTA sought to change that. Over the past 2 years the CTA has consistently shared more actionable threat intelligence such as information on zero-day vulnerabilities, command-and-control server information, mobile threats, and indicators of compromise related to advanced threats. By raising the industry's collective intelligence through these new data exchanges, CTA members have delivered greater security for individual customers and organizations. In short, the CTA is not about one vendor trying to gain advantage—we are all contributing and sharing with the community.

It is important to note that we have done this while maintaining the privacy of all our customer data and in full compliance with our companies' respective privacy policies. At Symantec, we take very seriously our obligation to protect our customers' privacy and maintain the confidentiality of the data they choose to share with us, and our analysts are rigorous in ensuring that all shared data is anonymized. In the digital world, security and privacy are intertwined, and the CTA is operational proof that the two can complement each other.

The CTA has worked because there are minimum contribution requirements for all members. Each must share at least 1,000 samples of new Portable Executable (PE) malware per day that were not otherwise seen over the preceding 48 hours. Further, they must provide one or more additional sets of data relating either to mobile malware samples, command-and-control servers, or vulnerabilities. Member company analysts meet every month to exchange information and plan joint reports, and the company CEOs meet quarterly. When the group decides to work on a research paper, company analysts work together more frequently—often several times a week just before publication.

The CTA's recent research paper on the Cryptowall ransomware trojan is a good example of what high-impact information sharing can bring. Each member shared their Indicators of Compromise (IOCs) around a particular threat, filling in intelligence gaps and allowing an expanded understanding of the criminal networks and their methods of operation. In addition to the research paper, the effort led to more comprehensive protection for all of our customers.

Efforts like the Cryptowall paper, of course, require significant resources from the member companies. And while members work together on research, they also compete in the marketplace. But the CTA has shown that with the proper planning and due care for company-specific considerations, even competitors can come together and raise the security level for all internet users.

CONCLUSION

The cyber threat landscape is always evolving—but so too are new security technologies. Cyber criminals will always seek new ways to compromise computers, but that does not mean they are always winning. In fact, we see attackers trying new techniques such as zero-day exploits because protection has become difficult to evade. These criminals did not invest the time and resources to develop new attack methods because they wanted too, they did it because they had too—because consumers were spotting their scams and security tools were blocking them. With cybersecurity, the old adage is true—there is no destination, just a journey. By driving up the cost of doing business for criminals we can make their journey all the more difficult and less lucrative. Symantec appreciates the committee's on-going interest in cybersecurity, and we look forward to continuing to work with you in the future.

Mr. RATCLIFFE. Thank you, Mr. Bromwich. The Chair now recognizes Dr. Porche for his opening statement.

STATEMENT OF ISAAC R. PORCHE, III, ASSOCIATE DIRECTOR, FORCES AND LOGISTICS PROGRAM, THE RAND ARMY RESEARCH DIVISION, THE RAND COMPANY

Mr. PORCHE. Thank you. Chairman Ratcliffe, Ranking Member Richmond, distinguished Members of the subcommittee, thank you for inviting me to this important discussion on cyber space and cybersecurity.

Let me start—since the creation of the internet's predecessor, the ARPANET, kaleidoscopic change has been the single constant in the information environment. What started out as a relatively wonky communications tool for a small group of scientists and engineers is now a global information infrastructure.

Information and communications technology changes rapidly, and it is difficult for even nimble corporations to keep up with modifications to stop the next threat or to close the next discovered vulnerability.

The challenge for the U.S. Government in cyber space is even greater. First, I discuss two trends that are driving this challenge. The first trend is that cyber space, which is expanding every day as more and more devices are brought on-line, is becoming increasingly vulnerable as cybersecurity resources are stretched thin. We are straining to keep pace with the increasing complexity as new devices come to the market and become interconnected. Meanwhile, cyber space is hosting increasingly vast amounts of data.

A metaphoric term, cyber space is like a balloon. It is constantly being filled with air, and constantly trying to prick the balloon are considerable numbers of people and organizations, terrorists, nation-states. This is the second trend. To continue with the metaphor, pins are like a dime a dozen. To deal with this, we need cybersecurity professionals working on building a tougher skin for the balloon, taking pins off the market, tracking down and stopping would-be pin-prickers.

But aside from hiring more professionals, what are the options for improving cybersecurity? In earlier RAND work that I published, we identify two needs. The first, enable substantially better information sharing and collaboration among key departments and agencies in the private sector. The Cybersecurity Information-Sharing Act of 2015 was needed, but small and careful step towards this goal. So why is sharing discovered vulnerabilities, defensive measures and best practices so important? Because bad actors benefit from slow identification and slow mitigation of the threat.

Given the time taken to identify a malicious intrusion and determine its extent, which is usually measured in months, the bad actors are long gone, along with your data. If Government entities and the private sector are sharing information quickly and often, they have a better chance of being able to anticipate and prepare for the eventual attack.

Also we have to go beyond just identifying and responding to attacks more quickly. Threats have to be anticipated. The behavior of threat actors has to be identified. Intelligence on threat actors and their intentions is a necessary ingredient to significantly improve the chances of predicting and identifying the next attack.

A challenge for achieving this kind of information sharing is co-operation, and much of the public is simply not comfortable with the idea of mass Government surveillance. Specific attitudes towards this issue are nuanced and complex, but the Pew Research Center reported 65 percent of U.S. adults believe that there are not adequate limits on the internet data that the Government collects. Frankly, even the most well-meaning proposals to increase information sharing between the Government and the private sector come across to some as something out of Orwell's "1984."

Public debate and discussion of how to balance the needs of security and privacy is a critical step. Information sharing is one perpetual need. A second is to achieve unity of effort across the U.S. Government, where different agencies and different organizations have different cyber responsibilities. Cyber defense requires a coherent response and the bureaucratic swim lines don't always contribute to synergy for that goal.

Ultimately, perhaps ideally what is needed is the ability to track cyber intruders, criminals, and other hostile actors with the same freedom of maneuver and speed these adversaries enjoy in cyber space today. Achieving this goal will required sustained, long-term efforts to develop policy and technology.

At present, many ideas for using technology to improve cybersecurity, such as pooling and mining vast stores of data, alarm all of us who believe in a right to privacy from Government intrusion, and perhaps new authorities will be required to make this happen. There also needs to be appreciation that everyone has a role to play in improving cybersecurity—the U.S. Government, developers and purveyors of internet-connected software and hardware, and individual consumers.

In conclusion, there is no simple solution to the threat posed by adversaries in cyber space, but one critical challenge that must be overcome is to determine how to protect the cybersecurity of a democratic society that demands both freedom and privacy in its use of computer systems and networks from the threats posed by enemies who respect no boundaries, who can act largely with impunity, and despite National and international norms and legal frameworks.

The ideas for commissions to discuss security and privacy are forward-thinking proposals, being put forth both by Congress and by the President, and I look forward to learning more about the details of these efforts.

Regarding current events, it is fair to say that today's debate about whether device-makers should be required to build backdoors into operating systems so law enforcement can collect data has jump-started this much-needed discussion. This kind of public debate is a good thing.

Thank you for your time, and I am happy to answer questions.

[The prepared statement of Dr. Porche follows:]

PREPARED STATEMENT OF ISAAC R. PORCHE, III[1][2]

FEBRUARY 25, 2016

Chairman Ratcliffe, Ranking Member Richmond, and Members of the subcommittee, thank you for inviting me to address important emerging concerns related to cyber space and cybersecurity. Specifically, I will discuss how cyber space continues to change, expand, and remain inherently vulnerable. I will discuss both the kind of information sharing that is needed to help defend cyber space proactively and how the public's privacy concerns affect that very information sharing. Finally, I will mention the needed next steps, including more discussion of the need to balance security and privacy, potential technological approaches, and the potential need for future legislation.

INTRODUCTION

Since the creation of the ARPANet—the internet's predecessor—kaleidoscopic change has been the single constant of the information environment. What started out as a relatively wonky communications tool for a smallish group of engineers, scientists, and computer experts is now a global information infrastructure: "a worldwide broadcasting capability, a mechanism for information dissemination, and a medium for collaboration and interaction between individuals and their computers without regard for geographic location."[3]

Today, it is useful to think of the information environment as two partially intersecting areas: Social networks and cyber space (Figure 1). Social networks are the webs of interactions and relationships among individuals. They are continuing to grow in size, relevance, and influence, affecting not only how we communicate with one another but if and how we find employment, housing, and romantic relationships; but social networks are also influencing the evolution of modern conflict. The so-called Islamic State, for example, has successfully used the social-networking platform Twitter to persuade distant potential recruits to literally—physically—mobilize.

"Cyber space is the technical foundation on which the world relies to interact, exchange information, conduct business, and so on. It is, according to the Joint Chiefs

---

[1] The opinions and conclusions expressed in this testimony are the author's alone and should not be interpreted as representing those of RAND or any of the sponsors of its research. This product is part of the RAND Corporation testimony series. RAND testimonies record testimony presented by RAND associates to Federal, State, or local legislative committees; Government-appointed commissions and panels; and private review and oversight bodies. The RAND Corporation is a nonprofit research organization providing objective analysis and effective solutions that address the challenges facing the public and private sectors around the world. RAND's publications do not necessarily reflect the opinions of its research clients and sponsors.

[2] This testimony is available for free download at *http://www.rand.org/pubs/testimonies/CT453.html*.

[3] Barry M. Leiner, Vinton G. Cerf, David D. Clark, Robert E. Kahn, Leonard Kleinrock, Daniel C. Lynch, Jon Postel, Larry G. Roberts, and Stephen Wolff, "Brief History of the Internet," InternetSociety.org, undated.

of Staff, a global domain within the information environment consisting of the inter-dependent networks of information technology infrastructures and resident data, including the internet, telecommunications networks, computer systems, and embedded processors and controllers."[4]

Cyber space is both a global domain and a global commons whose reach is being constantly expanded not only by wired and wireless connections, but by sneaker-netted connectors that close all air gaps.[5] Everything from home thermostats to the critical infrastructure that is vital to daily life—water, power, manufacturing, etc.— is within its reach. It is "shared by all" and currently dominated by none. Eventually, controlling cyber space (and the intersecting electromagnetic spectrum) could be tantamount to controlling the information environment.

Figure 1. The Information Environment Includes Social Networks and Cyberspace

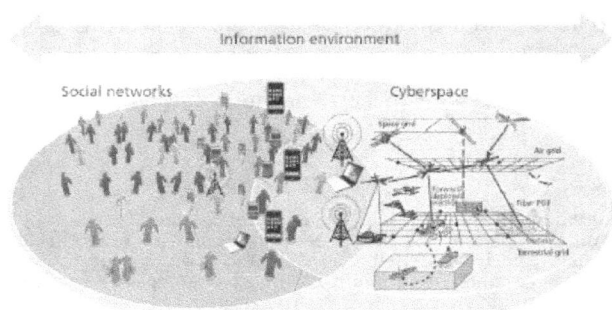

SOURCE: Isaac R. Porche III, Christopher Paul, Michael York, Chad C. Serena, Jerry M. Sollinger, Elliot Axelband, Endy M. Daehner, and Bruce J. Held, *Redefining Information Warfare Boundaries for an Army in a Wireless World*, Santa Monica, Calif.: RAND Corporation, MG-1113-A, 2013.

The rapid pace of change makes it difficult for even nimble corporations to keep up with emerging threats and to close newly-discovered vulnerabilities, and the challenge for the U.S. Government is even greater. Governmental controls and processes make rapidly acquiring materiel difficult, and it is also difficult to make rapid changes in personnel structure. Thus, keeping up with major changes, such as the merging of the wired and wireless worlds, poses formidable challenges to all.[6]

TWO TRENDS IN CYBER SPACE

For a moment, think of cyber space as a balloon that's constantly being filled with more and more air. As the balloon gets bigger, the amount of surface area that is vulnerable to a pinprick increases, the skin of the balloon stretches and gets thinner, and the volume of air trapped inside grows. I use the balloon metaphor to help illustrate three key points about today's cybersecurity environment:
- First, like the surface of the balloon, the "attack surface area" of cyber space is expanding every day as more and more devices are brought on-line. Some estimate that, right now, there are billions of internet-connected devices—a number that could surpass a trillion in just 10 years.[7] Each smartphone, computer,

---

[4] Joint Chiefs of Staff, Cyberspace Operations, Joint Publication 3–12R, February 5, 2013.

[5] *Sneakernet* is an informal term that describes using physical media (e.g., thumb drives, CDs) rather than a computer network to move electronic information from one computer to another.

[6] Most of the language and analysis in this section is drawn from Porche et al., 2013.

[7] Estimates vary. In 2014, Gartner, Inc., forecasted that 6.4 billion internet-connected devices would be in use world-wide in 2016, and that 20.8 billion would be in use by 2020. "In 2016," Gartner predicted, "5.5 million new things will get connected every day" ("Gartner Says 4.9 Billion Connected 'Things' Will Be in Use in 2015," *Gartner.com*, press release, November 11, 2014). In 2015, *Business Insider* estimated that 10 billion devices were connected world-wide and that 34 billion will be connected by 2020 (Jonathan Camhi, "BI Intelligence Projects 34 Billion Devices Will Be Connected by 2020," *BusinessInsider.com*, November 6, 2015). In 2015, Juniper Research suggested that the number of internet-connected devices will reach 38.5 billion in 2020 ("'Internet of Things' Connected Devices to Almost Triple to Over 38 Billion Units by 2020," *JuniperResearch.com*, press release, July 28, 2015). According to the 2016 Georgia Tech

tablet, television, refrigerator, and "intelligent" vehicle is a potential cyber target.

- Second, like the skin of the balloon, cybersecurity resources—which are already stretched thin—must try to keep pace with increasing complexity as new devices come to market and become interconnected. For example, if you upgrade your old home security system to a new one that connects to your smartphone, you have complicated the task of protecting your home by introducing several cyber vulnerabilities.
- Third, like the air inside the balloon, the amount and type of data we are all actively and passively uploading to the Internet is constantly expanding. One popular traffic app for smartphones constantly monitors your location, even when you are not using the app. You have to actively turn this feature off if you do not want your phone to share your location with the app—and with the app's partners—every single minute. The entire "digital universe" is already billions of terabytes and constantly growing. Estimates of the annual growth of this universe vary, but the increases appear to be exponential (see Figure 2).[8]

Figure 2. The Digital Universe Is Growing Exponentially

Estimated Size of the Digital Universe

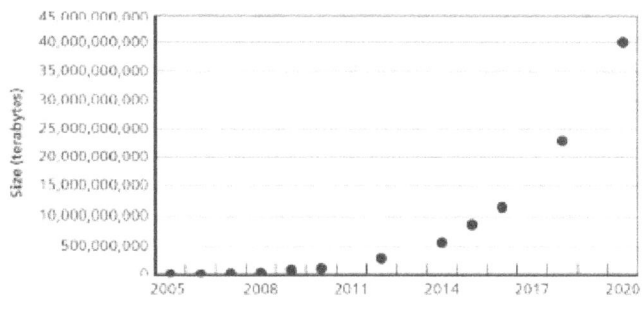

SOURCE: Porche et al., 2014.

So, cyber space is expanding, becoming increasingly vulnerable, and hosting increasingly vast amounts of (sometimes critical) data. That's the first trend. The second trend is that the number of bad actors seeking to exploit cyber space for criminal or malicious purposes is growing too: "Since the mid-2000s," RAND Corporation experts warn, "the hacking community has been steadily growing and maturing."[9] In 2014, more than a billion personal data records were compromised by cyber attacks—a 78 percent "surge" in the number of personal data records compromised compared with 2013.[10]

Considerable numbers of people and organizations—including highly organized groups with cartel, terrorist, or even nation-state connections[11]—are constantly trying to prick the balloon, and pins are a dime a dozen. Tools for bad actors in cyber space are, quite literally, commodities:

Emerging Cyber Threats Report, there could be a trillion devices by 2025 (Institute for Information Security and Privacy, *Emerging Cyber Threats Report 2016*, Georgia Institute of Technology, 2015).

[8] The estimates and projections in the section are drawn from Isaac R. Porche III, Bradley Wilson, Erin-Elizabeth Johnson, Shane Tierney, and Evan Saltzman, *Data Flood: Helping the Navy Address the Rising Tide of Sensor Information*, Santa Monica, Calif.: RAND Corporation, RR–315–NAVY, 2014.

[9] Lillian Ablon, Martin C. Libicki, and Andrea A. Golay, *Markets for Cybercrime Tools and Stolen Data: Hackers' Bazaar*, Santa Monica, Calif.: RAND Corporation, RR–610–JNI, 2014.

[10] Arjun Kharpal, "Year of the Hack? A Billion Records Compromised in 2014," *CNBC.com*, February 12, 2015.

[11] Ablon, Libicki, and Golay, 2014.

They can be—and are being—bought and sold. For example, cyber criminals have sold login credentials for Facebook in bulk,[12] even as more and more sites are encouraging users to log in using their Facebook accounts. Training in malicious hacking can be acquired easily and for free on-line on sites you probably visit a few times a week, like YouTube. Experts agree that the coming years will bring more activity in so-called darknets, and more use of crypto-currencies; that the ability to stage cyber attacks will continue to outpace the ability to defend against them;[13] and that there will be more hacking for hire.[14] Furthermore, a body of research is emerging called automatic exploit generation (AEG) that seeks algorithms that automatically generate large quantities of exploitable bugs.[15]

WHY THESE TRENDS IN CYBER SPACE WILL PERSIST

A number of factors guarantee that cyber space will continue to expand, continue to become increasingly vulnerable, and continue to host increasingly vast amounts of (sometimes critical) data:

- the shift to digitized information (e.g., voice, video, and data)
- the miniaturization of computing and data-storage devices that carry digitized information, coupled with low costs, which has fostered an explosion of increasingly networked digital devices
- continued growth in wired and wireless networks and electronic systems, which make it possible to access, via the internet, systems that used to be isolated (i.e., off-line)
- the accelerating deployment of digital control systems that operate physical systems, from cars to aircraft, from home thermostats to the power grid, and so on
- the increasing popularity of on-line media and social networking, which, according to one study, has led some people to spend more time each day on a phone or laptop (an average of 8 hours and 41 minutes) than sleeping[16]
- the combined decrease in cost, increase in speed, and standardization of inter-operating electronic systems, which not only make these systems more accessible to anyone but also increase the potential for exploitation.

These and other trends enable any government or state to use capabilities that were once available only to developed countries with large defense budgets, although it should be noted that these capabilities simultaneously increase the exposure of those countries. Additionally, individuals who were previously considered noncombatants can now join the battle and wage silent, electronic war. Finally, as information systems become ubiquitous, our reliance on them increases apace. Today's modern economic, political, and military systems depend more than ever on information and instructions generated in cyber space nodes and transmitted across a vast network. Such reliance invites conflict and exploitation.

OPTIONS TO ADDRESS THE EMERGING LANDSCAPE IN CYBER SPACE AND OBSTACLES TO IMPLEMENTING THEM

So, who do we have working on building a tougher skin for the balloon, taking pins off the market, and tracking down and stopping would-be pin-prickers? We have good guys: Cybersecurity professionals, "white hat" hackers, and other individuals who are identifying and patching vulnerabilities and who are trying to take down the bad actors. However, at the moment, in the U.S. Government, there sim-

---

[12] Amit Klein, "Fraudsters Selling Login Credentials for Facebook, Twitter in Bulk," *SecurityIntelligence.com,* February 8, 2012.

[13] This is a viewpoint echoed by former Deputy Secretary of Defense William Lynn in Foreign Affairs: "In cyber space, the offense has the upper hand . . . [T]he U.S. Government's ability to defend its networks always lags behind its adversaries' ability to exploit U.S. networks' weaknesses . . . In an offense-dominant environment, a fortress mentality will not work. (William J. Lynn III, "Defending a New Domain: The Pentagon's Cyberstrategy," *Foreign Affairs,* September/October 2010.)

[14] Ablon, Libicki, and Golay, 2014.

[15] According to Matthew Ruffell's overview of AEG (Matthew Ruffell, "Applying Bytecode Level Automatic Exploit Generation to Embedded Systems," Christchurch, New Zealand: University of Canterbury, October 16, 2015), Brumley et al. discovered in 2008 that it was possible to automatically generate an exploit by analyzing a vulnerable binary program and the patched binary program by comparing the two and pinpointing what code had been changed and ultimately output an exploit. See David Brumley, Pongsin Poosankam, Dawn Song, and Jiang Zheng, "Automatic Patch-Based Exploit Generation Is Possible: Techniques and Implications," *IEEE Symposium on Security and Privacy, 2008,* May 18–22, 2008, pp. 143–157.

[16] Madlen Davies, "Average Person Now Spends More Time on Their Phone and Laptop than Sleeping, Study Claims," *DailyMail.co.uk,* March 11, 2015.

ply are not enough of these good guys to go around.[17] Educating, recruiting, training, and hiring cybersecurity professionals takes time, and the most-capable professionals—the elite commercial "cyber ninjas"—can command salaries that the Government simply cannot match.[18]

Aside from hiring more good guys, what are our options for improving cybersecurity? One of the best options is improving information sharing and cooperation between and among Government entities and the private sector. The Cybersecurity Information Sharing Act of 2015, which contains elements to help facilitate information sharing, is one effort that could stimulate the kind of information sharing that is needed.[19] Why is sharing of discovered vulnerabilities, defense measures, and best practices so important? Because bad actors benefit from slow identification and slow mitigation of a threat.[20] Given the time taken to identify a malicious intrusion and determine its extent, which is usually measured in months, the bad actors are long gone, along with your data.[21] If Government entities and the private sector were sharing information quickly and often, they have a better chance of being able to anticipate and prepare for an eventual attack. So, beyond just identifying and responding to attacks more quickly, threats have to be anticipated and the behavior of threat actors known. Intelligence on threat actors and their intentions is a necessary ingredient to significantly improve the chances of predicting and identifying the next act.

Unfortunately, several factors make this kind of information sharing and cooperation a lot easier to talk about than to actually implement. First is the fact that cyber space is largely a private-sector construct, subject to private-sector concerns. Working against the pursuit of perfect (or even good-enough) security is the need to get software and hardware to the market quickly, at a competitive price, and with all the innovative features none of us yet know that we absolutely cannot live without. As of June 2015, developers were submitting more than 1,000 apps to Apple every day for evaluation.[22] At that kind of volume, Apple cannot be expected to validate that every single app it approves is perfectly secure—no matter how it is used, no matter what other apps the user runs, and whether those apps are updated as needed. The result is a sprawling universe of software and hardware, some of which is, as the 2016 National threat assessment put it, "designed and fielded with minimal security requirements and testing . . . [such that they] could lead to widespread vulnerabilities in civilian infrastructure and [U.S. Government] systems."[23]

The second obstacle to this kind of information sharing and cooperation is that most of the U.S. public is simply not comfortable with the idea of mass Government surveillance. Specific attitudes toward this issue are nuanced and complex, but the Pew Research Center reported that, in 2015, 65 percent of U.S. adults believed that "there are not adequate limits on the telephone and internet data that the government collects."[24] Frankly, even the most well-meaning proposals to increase information sharing between the Government and the private sector can feel like something out of George Orwell's *1984*.

However, despite private-sector imperatives and public concerns about a "Big Brother" nation, there are real, serious threats to, from, and in cyber space: Threats to American citizens, American businesses, and critical National infrastructure. It will be increasingly difficult for the U.S. Government, along with State and local agencies—including law enforcement—to pursue and prosecute cyber criminals and other nefarious actors without some kind of continued information sharing and co-

---

[17] Joe Davidson, "Lack of Digital Talent Adds to Cybersecurity Problems," *Washington Post,* July 19, 2015.

[18] Martin C. Libicki, David Senty, and Julia Pollak, *Hackers Wanted: An Examination of the Cybersecurity Labor Market,* Santa Monica, Calif.: RAND Corporation, RR–430, 2014.

[19] This includes sharing of knowledge about cybersecurity threats (including vulnerabilities), indicators of cybersecurity threats (e.g., malicious reconnaissance), and sharing of defensive measures and best practices.

[20] Many attacks come after the announcement of a vulnerability and release of a patch: "When software vendors announce and ship patches, hackers analyze the patches and can often develop exploits for the problem faster than companies can install the patch" (James A. Lewis, *Raising the Bar for Cybersecurity,* Washington, DC: Center for Strategic and International Studies, February 12, 2013).

[21] According to Mandiant's 2015 threat report, *A View from the Front Lines,* the median duration that threat groups were present on a victim's network before detection was 205 days.

[22] Jerin Matthew, "Apple App Store Growing by Over 1,000 Apps per Day," *IBITimes.co.uk,* June 6, 2015.

[23] James R. Clapper, Director of National Intelligence, "Statement for the Record: Worldwide Threat Assessment of the U.S. Intelligence Community," presented to the Senate Armed Services Committee, February 9, 2016.

[24] Mary Madden and Lee Rainie, "Americans' Attitudes About Privacy, Security, and Surveillance," *PewInternet.org,* May 20, 2015.

operation that has occurred routinely in the past. The likely court fight emerging now between the Federal Bureau of Investigation and Apple over unlocking the phone of one of the San Bernardino attackers is a timely example. It is worrisome to privacy advocates that are concerned that this is a "test case for the general principle that [the Government] should be able to compel tech companies to assist in police investigations."[25]

BUREAUCRATIC AND LEGAL ISSUES THAT CAN HAMPER DEFENSE

Defending against sophisticated attacks against critical infrastructure (such as Stuxnet, a computer "worm" allegedly designed to sabotage Iran's nuclear program) requires excellent capabilities marshaled into a coherent and coordinated response. The United States has plenty of the former but, in my view, has difficulty conducting the latter. Responsibilities can overlap or conflict. For example, stealing financial information is a crime, and the Federal Bureau of Investigation is charged with dealing with such criminal activity. However, the Department of Homeland Security has a mandate to protect the civilian agencies of the Federal Executive branch and to lead the protection of critical cyber space.[26]

Good intelligence has always been a prerequisite to good defense, but many attacks come from overseas locations. Therefore, efforts to garner intelligence outside the United States would involve the agencies authorized to do so. Many regard the National Security Agency as the most capable Government entity when it comes to analyzing and defending against cyber attacks. But legal limits constrain what the U.S. Department of Defense and intelligence community can do. Much illicit activity masks itself in emails, but privacy laws preclude how much the Government can monitor such transmissions.

None of this is to say that these carefully defined limitations cannot be overcome. Indeed, a number of proposed pieces of legislation attempt to deal with them. However, the challenge is great and is compounded by the speed needed to respond to increasingly sophisticated threats. Worms can be scrubbed from systems if its administrators know the systems have been breached. But they need to act within the window of opportunity, whether that is days, weeks, or months. Otherwise, the worm will have done its damage and then erased itself.[27]

THE WAY AHEAD

To better prepare to mitigate the emerging threats and improve the cybersecurity of this country, two overarching goals should be pursued continuously:

- First, enable substantially better information sharing and collaboration among key departments and agencies (Department of Justice, Department of Homeland Security, Department of Defense, and Office of the Director of National Intelligence) and the private sector. The Cybersecurity Information Sharing Act of 2015 was a needed, but small and careful, step toward this goal, in part because it encourages the private sector (via liability protections) and U.S. Government to share knowledge of cybersecurity threats, including Classified vulnerabilities, best practices, and defensive measures. This law could better enable the community to anticipate attacks and have a more proactive defense posture.
- Second, achieve unity of effort across the U.S. Government. Today, different Government agencies have different cyber responsibilities. This makes perfect sense in many ways, because different agencies have different capabilities, so they should be tasked to do what they are good at doing. The trick is to harness all the capabilities to a common end, and therein lies the problem. Cyber defense requires a coherent response, and the bureaucratic responsibilities as currently articulated hinder progress toward that goal. President Obama's appointment of a Chief Information Security Officer for the country—part of his newly-

---

[25] Ben Adida, "On Apple and the FBI," *Benlog.com* blog post, February 18, 2016.

[26] Further, the Defense Department has responsibility for defending U.S. National interests against cyber attacks of "significant consequence."

[27] The language and analysis in this section is drawn from Isaac R. Porche, Jerry M. Sollinger and Shawn McKay, *A Cyberworm that Knows No Boundaries*, Santa Monica, Calif.: RAND Corporation, OP–342–OSD, 2011.

announced Cybersecurity National Action Plan[28]—is another careful small step toward some needs.[29]

Ultimately, perhaps ideally, what is needed is the ability to track cyber intruders, criminals, and other hostile actors in cyber space with the same freedom of maneuver (and speed) these adversaries enjoy. Achieving this goal will require a sustained, long-term effort. New authorities will be required, along with substantial revisions to the U.S. Code (a daunting challenge). Public debate will be lively. Indeed, I have long argued that public debate is a critical first step:

"Government intrusion into private affairs, even for reasons of the common defense, evokes an emotional response . . . A first step requires an honest, public debate [that] calls into question the very firewalls between public and private sectors that are intrinsic to democracy."[30]

Furthermore, what is needed is a discussion of how to best balance the need for security and privacy. There are many ways to facilitate this kind of discussion, and the proposal put forth by Full Committee Chairman Michael McCaul and Senator Mark Warner is one way to move forward, though there could be others.

It is fair say that today's debate about whether device makers should be required to build "back doors" into operating systems so law enforcement and intelligence agencies can collect data has jump-started this much-needed discussion. This is a good thing.

In the short term, the next steps are multipronged. Congress needs to continue to develop strong, smart policies and laws designed to improve cybersecurity—laws like the Cybersecurity Information Sharing Act of 2015. Although there is an immediate need for such policies and laws, Congress would be well-advised to incrementally design these policies and laws, and communicate them to the public, to earn the public's confidence in the Government's ability and intentions. Specifically, the public must be convinced that the Government's information needs are balanced with individuals' desire for privacy. At present, many ideas for, and approaches to, using technology to improve cybersecurity—such as pooling and mining vast stores of data—alarm those who believe in a right to privacy from Government intrusion.[31]

There also needs to be appreciation that everyone has a role to play in improving cybersecurity:

- *The U.S. Government* should continue to facilitate and encourage information sharing and cooperation between and among Government entities and the private sector to protect citizens, businesses, and critical infrastructure against cyber threats. Department of Homeland Security Secretary Jeh Johnson has just recently announced preliminary guidance for information sharing between the private sector and the U.S. Government.[32] Eventually, the U.S. Government should also find ways to exploit all forms of data and intelligence to identify and anticipate both threats and bad actors, without unacceptably infringing on individuals' desire for privacy.
- *Developers and purveyors* of internet-connected software and hardware—including large corporations, individual app developers, and everyone in between—need to be equipped to understand the security impacts of their work.[33] Today, a software developer does not need to have a degree, or any formal training, or any license whatsoever to write programs that control our infrastructure. There are few, if any, engineering fields that find themselves in a similar predicament. For example, the design of a drawbridge requires the oversight and approval of a licensed civil engineer, whereas anyone, in theory, can design the

---

[28] 28 The White House, Office of the Press Secretary, "Fact Sheet: Cybersecurity National Action Plan," February 9, 2016. A related news article noted that "the Obama administration is creating a new high-level federal official to coordinate cybersecurity across civilian agencies and to work with military and intelligence counterparts, as part of its 2017 budget proposal announced Tuesday" (Tami Abdollah, "Obama Administration Plans New High-Level Cyber Official," *ABCNews.com*, February 9, 2016).

[29] For example, Government information technology modernization.

[30] Isaac Porche, "Stuxnet Is the World's Problem," *Bulletin of the Atomic Scientists*, December 19, 2010.

[31] For example, big data analytics in support of cybersecurity.

[32] Aaron Boyd, "DHS Releases Initial Guidelines for Cyber Threat Info-Sharing," *FederalTimes.com*, February 17, 2016.

[33] Threats and vulnerabilities can originate anywhere, including the usual suspects (e.g., known hackers) or even well-intentioned amateur code writers. A malicious hacker with a laptop and a seat in an internet café has everything needed to launch an attack in cyber space. Alternatively, a well-intentioned but naïve "app writer" can accidentally propagate a useful utility that unlocks backdoor access.

software that controls that bridge. Cybersecurity is everyone's responsibility, from the chief information security officer to the individual app developer.[34]
- *Individual consumers* should do more to protect their software, hardware, and private information. Simply put, most of us are either too busy or insufficiently educated (likely both) to spend our days and nights patching every device in the home. We often keep old and impossible-to-secure devices and computers up and running. As the President's Cybersecurity National Action Plan notes, there is too much old, outdated equipment on-line today, which makes for easily targeted entry points and "botnet soldiers."[35]

There is no simple solution to the threat posed by adversaries in cyber space. However, one critical challenge that must be overcome—soon—is determining how to protect the cybersecurity of a democratic society that demands both freedom and privacy in its use of computer systems and networks from the threat posed by enemies who respect no boundaries and can act largely with impunity, despite National and international norms and legal frameworks.

Thank you for your time and I am happy to answer any questions.

Mr. RATCLIFFE. Thank you, Dr. Porche. I now recognize the gentleman from Pennsylvania, Mr. Marino, for 5 minutes of questions.

Mr. MARINO. Thank you, Chairman. Good afternoon, and thank you all for being here.

I am going to ask a couple questions that I would like each of you to respond to, so maybe we could start with Mr. Cilluffo, please. I am constantly doing town hall meetings and meet with businesses and even individuals, and I am amazed at the number of people in corporations that really do not understand what can happen to their personal computers, to their business operations, and so forth.

So we need to somehow ramp up the ability to educate the public. How do we do that?

Mr. CILLUFFO. Congressman Marino, that is an excellent question, and I think it is one we are all struggling with here. But unfortunately, I think there are enough recent incidents where—shame on us if we keep hitting that snooze button, whether it is the Hollywood Presbyterian example—this is an example where you had individuals' medical records locked up, and it actually had actual operational effect on the OR and the emergency room of the hospital. It had real impact.

The cyber attack in the Ukraine on the grid, this actually—people didn't have power. So these are no longer zeros and ones that are invisible to average citizens, but we are starting to see that cyber attacks affect not only the cyber domain, but the physical domain and the physical world.

That said, right now, intellectual property theft is probably the most rampant concern that we all have. Businesses realize that. Unfortunately in your own State, some realize that when it was too late.

Mr. MARINO. Okay. Ms. Kolde, how do we educate people?

Ms. KOLDE. Thank you. I think that the education needs to occur across all levels of education, in terms of cyber education, as well as all levels of the business organizational infrastructure. I think we need greater awareness among individual computer users of the risks of on-line operations, doing your banking on-line and so forth,

---

[34] Many technology companies insist that they have to train all new employees, whether hired with a degree or not, on techniques for secure development. There is a gap in our educational system at all levels.
[35] The White House, Office of the Press Secretary, 2016.

and what you can do to protect yourself and your identity and your financial assets.

From the corporate or the organizational standpoint, there needs to be additional education at the business level, the management level, of the risks to business. Cyber is one additional risk that any corporation faces and should be taken into account, along with other operational risks that a business must deal with.

In addition, we need better education across technical personnel, those who are charged with managing information systems and securing networks, as to both best practices and the potential risks that can occur to that organization and ways to defend against them.

Mr. MARINO. Okay, I am going to switch now because I only have a couple minutes. But wouldn't it be a good idea for every laptop, phone, desktop computer that is put out there, that the industry can agree on some type of short learning introduction on that computer before you start doing anything that someone has to read and pay attention to? Just a thought.

Mr. BROMWICH. Yes, actually I was going to answer that kind of question, actually, which is I think there is been a big focus on— I think on attacks in the news. I think the public understands the attacks, but they don't understand at all the technologies that they need to have, like multi-factor authentication.

These technologies are actually fairly simple and straightforward. They can be made easy to adopt. I think it is a matter of the public understanding—telling the public, communicating to the public how important it is to adopt these technologies.

I think we can educate consumers on these attacks more, but ultimately the technology has to be there to do the protection for them. I don't think it is enough to ask a consumer to always just be vigilant or, you know, change their password frequently. We need to provide them the technologies that make this a seamless process.

Mr. MARINO. Dr. Porche, I want to switch to a question that shoots off this. What is the Federal Government's ability or lack thereof to address, prevent, and/or curtail a cyber attack on a large scale?

Mr. PORCHE. I think the Federal Government has strengths that affect everyone in this country, in that the Federal Government has information and resources to gather about what the threats are. One of the themes in my testimony was—or at least I tried to put forth—is get in front of the threat, anticipate what is going to happen. Your success goes up so much higher when you have a better idea of what is coming around the pike, as opposed to a simple reaction. I don't know anybody else who can help with that concept.

Also as came out in the CISA 2015 bill, sort of a clearinghouse that DHS can play in gathering all the information that can be spread out. I mean, no one has the power to gather the information more than the Federal Government, and no one is in a position to have to protect it more carefully because of the power of the Federal Government. So it is a good balancing act. But the resources of the Federal Government to gather information are incredible.

Mr. MARINO. Thank you. I yield back.

Mr. RATCLIFFE. I thank the gentleman. The Chair now recognizes the Ranking Minority Member of the subcommittee, Mr. Richmond, for his questions.

Mr. RICHMOND. Thank you. I would address it to Dr. Porche, and if any other Members want to comment on it, that is fine. Dr. Porche, you know that my district probably in terms of critical infrastructure, we have 3 major sea ports, we have probably the largest petrochemical footprint of any district in the country, we have major cross-country pipelines, and then we have major interstate and rail, and with all different owners and players that control each.

So I guess the question is, what are some of the unique cybersecurity challenges that critical infrastructure owners and operators face? Are there any particular emerging cyber threats that are unique to critical infrastructure?

Mr. PORCHE. Yes, sir, thank you. Growing up in Baton Rouge, down the street from the Exxon refinery plant, I am intimately aware of the critical infrastructure and what can happen there.

There are some unique things about critical infrastructure. For one, although it is not a popular target for people trying to make a profit, that is good and bad, because the flipside is that the people who—the adversaries who are interested in potentially targeting critical infrastructure could potentially be more sophisticated adversaries.

So critical infrastructure today might have to deal with a more sophisticated threat than, let's say, a hardware store might have to, although the impact could be the same in terms of what could happen.

The other issue with critical infrastructure is, you know, there could be vulnerabilities planted or just designed in that exist for years before they are noticed. Critical infrastructure may employ things like programmable logic controllers and older equipment that is not the latest PC, and so now you are dealing with a different way to protect different types of information technology.

So awareness of what is going on in that critical infrastructure is vital. Understanding what is normal and what is abnormal is critical and help, because the critical infrastructure needs to be protected from potentially skillful adversaries who have resources.

Mr. RICHMOND. Anyone want to comment or——

Mr. BROMWICH. Yes, I would just say that the protection that critical infrastructure needs is slightly different from what a typically enterprise would need, and so it actually raises the bar for critical infrastructure. They have to be a lot more educated and knowledgeable about the technology. Today, they are taking common Windows computers and using them for really important tasks, when they could be really narrowing down the technology they use and reducing the attack surface. So that is an important consideration for critical infrastructure.

Mr. CILLUFFO. Mr. Richmond, a couple of other quick thoughts. I mean, industrial control systems, which are agnostic to a particular critical infrastructure, this is an area where you are seeing a major spike in activity. The good news is, is that the energy sector writ large and the electric sector in particular is doing some good work with their information-sharing and analysis centers, but they are not as far along as, say, the financial services sector is, where you have the Financial Services Information-Sharing and Analysis Center, the FSISAC, where they are actually sharing information in real-time to do patches and the like through tools that are referred to as STIX and TAXII that the Department of Homeland Security and others have made available to the private sector.

So I do think that the good news is, is they recognize obviously the implications and the impact. The bad news is, is the threat vector is expanding, the attack surface is growing, and quite honestly, the greatest solution in my eyes will be to bake security into the design of the infrastructures itself.

So the more you can think about this on the front end, rather than Lego and attaching security on the back end, would be money and time well spent.

Mr. RICHMOND. You mentioned that they are not where the financial services sector is in terms of information sharing, collaboration and all of that. What do you think we need to do to get them there? Do you think we have to do it through legislation incentives, you know, stick or carrot? I mean, what do you think?

Mr. CILLUFFO. I am always for carrots before sticks, so I do think there are some innovative approaches we can examine in terms of tax incentives and other means in the like. I know that is a very difficult and politically charged set of issues, but I don't think the regulatory check the box—that is looking through rear-view mirrors. It is looking at what we saw yesterday.

The reality is, is the bad guys are thinking ahead, and they are learning from our mistakes. They are learning from their own mistakes, their own dry runs. They are consistently learning and adapting their tactics and techniques.

So I do think the reason the financial services sector stepped up is the old Willie Sutton principle. Why rob banks? That is where the money is. They are getting hit. They feel it. It hits their bottom line. It impacts confidence and trust.

Clearly, I think with the energy sector and when you are looking at the potential implications from a public safety standpoint, that ought to also be at the top of the list. But I think first we want to see them come together as an organization, and like I said, there has been some real momentum. I don't want to take away from that, but not as far along as the financial services sector.

Mr. RICHMOND. Thank you, and I yield back.

Mr. RATCLIFFE. Thank the gentleman. The Chair now welcomes and recognizes the Chairman of the full committee, Mr. McCaul.

Chairman MCCAUL. Thank you, Mr. Chairman. I ask unanimous consent that my statement be put into the record.

Mr. RATCLIFFE. Without objection, so ordered.

[The statement of Chairman McCaul follows:]

STATEMENT OF CHAIRMAN MICHAEL T. MCCAUL

FEBRUARY 25, 2016

Our country is under constant attack from adversaries seeking access to our critical infrastructure and personal data. They are using our own information systems against us. The reality is this: The web has become a weapon, and nation states, criminal enterprises, and terrorist organizations are acting with increasing sophistication on the on-line battlefield. We must understand these cyber threats in order to protect our homeland against them.

Today, we expect to hear about the threats we face in today's cyber landscape. But I hope our witnesses will also discuss how America should confront them. We cannot stand on the sidelines while faceless enemies penetrate our networks. Nor can we afford to fail out of negligence or apathy. Our message to cyber assailants should be clear—America will not retreat; we will defend ourselves.

I applaud the President's recent Cybersecurity National Action Plan for proposing increased attention and resources to combat these threats. However, I still have questions about the overall strategy guiding these efforts. The administration must release the National Cybersecurity Incident Response plan, which is required by law in the National Cybersecurity Protection Act of 2014, which I sponsored. The administration says the plan will be out this spring, and I urge them to get it done.

The President's recent cyber proposal is an approach I have been pushing for us to adopt for more than a decade as a member of the Cybersecurity Caucus. I am disappointed, though, that it took until his last year in office for the President to release it. In cyber space, we know all-too-well that delay can be disastrous. We saw this with the OPM breach and the Sony Hack, and I fear that leadership lapses on the cyber front will have consequences for years to come.

I want to thank the witnesses for joining us today. It is disconcerting—but important—for us to hear the truth about the severity of the cyber challenges we face. We have not kept pace with our adversaries. If we want to disrupt their attacks, we must be vigilant and keep an eye toward the future. Above all else, our task must be to keep the American people safe.

Chairman MCCAUL. Thank you. I apologize, I am a little bit under the weather, but I find this topic fascinating. I agree, Frank, that we have to be in front of this, not trying to catch up to it.

I looked at the OPM breach and the fact that the Chinese were in our systems for somewhere—14 months to 2 years before we detected that, the fact that according to your testimony, you know, that Russia and Chinese actors have probably already penetrated our grid systems, that they may be actually sitting in the systems, at a point where they could turn it off.

I think the legislation we passed is helpful with information sharing, malicious codes. It will be interesting, it is a bit of an experiment to see how well it works. I just met with the CIO of JPMorgan about their efforts in the financial sector and also being able to share private-to-private with liability protection.

But I think that is something that the Congress can do, obviously. We have oversight. But I am interested in really, what kind of technologies do we see on the horizon? This is maybe where FireEye comes in. I got a briefing from FireEye yesterday, and iSIGHT. In terms of being able to see these threats before they penetrate or, if they do, be able to detect aberrant behavior within a network to shut down that actor and maybe firewall it off.

We know Mr. Snowden did great damage as a systems administrator. We know the OPM breach involved old credentials getting inside of the system, so that aberrant behavior is also another threat that I see. But I think, you know, we can pass a lot of laws, but I think—I mean, I am interested to hear, what kind of technology software systems do you see on the horizon?

Ms. KOLDE. Thank you. I think you have pointed out some very good examples, where traditionally in the past much of our security infrastructure has focused on protecting the perimeter and identifying attacks as they come into the network, or signature-based technology that relies on alerting things we already know about. So I think as we move forward and we evolve in terms to better protect our networks, those technologies have to do a couple of things.

One is to be able to engage detection after the fact. So once the attackers are already in your network, as they are moving from machine to machine, as they are attempting to escalate their privileges within the environment, how do we deploy technology that can detect that type of activity when it is not necessarily based on a specific signature or a previously known piece of malware?

We also have to enable our security defenders, those people who are responsible for modeling those networks, to better be able to triage the alerts that are occurring in their environment. If you have been a network analysis and you get thousands of alerts a day, how do you decide which of those alerts are the most worthy of your attention and the most important to respond to?

So context around alert data to help the responders prioritize is critical. Information sharing, as well. Some of what iSIGHT does is to proactively look at the threat landscape. What do we think criminal actors are going to do based on the chatter that we are hearing? What do we think that nation-states may attempt?

So getting more of that information out to the people who need it, to be a bit more predictive, would also be extremely helpful.

Chairman MCCAUL. Yes, and in our bill that we passed, we have the defense of Federal networks act in there. So you have to look at DHS and their ability to protect the dot-gov space, that is where I think the private sector really has a lot of the solutions.

I mean, Frank, do you have any comment on that?

Mr. CILLUFFO. Chairman McCaul, I think you raise a number of excellent points and clearly the ability to repel bad actors when they are in your system has to be part of that solution set.

But let me throw another idea out on the table, and I don't know if this is the right time and place. But we have seen major improvements in terms of information sharing. Kudos to all of you on the dais for moving legislation, as well.

The reality, though, is we have got to get beyond static information sharing. What I think we need to get to is where the private sector can drive intelligence requirements that the Government can help then glean and collect against.

So you are never going to get that family jewels, that secret sauce document. What you need to be able to do is the private sector needs to be able to levy what their specific requirements and needs are and then those that have collection capabilities to be able to meet those needs. I think that is the next level of discussion that we can translate some of the good work in terms of legislation into action.

Chairman MCCAUL. I appreciate that. I see my time has expired.

Mr. RATCLIFFE. Thank the gentleman. The Chair now recognizes the—oh, yes?

Mr. RICHMOND. Mr. Chairman, I would like to ask unanimous consent to enter into the record two letters of comments and also the Ranking Member's opening statement.

Mr. RATCLIFFE. Without objection, so ordered.

[The information follows:]

STATEMENT OF RANKING MEMBER BENNIE G. THOMPSON

FEBRUARY 25, 2016

Earlier this Congress, this subcommittee heard from the Federal Government in detail the roles that the Department of Homeland Security takes in its mission to secure information networks and provide resilience, not only to Government systems, but to assist private networks and data and protecting the Nation's critical infrastructure.

On February 16, the Department of Homeland Security along with the Department of Justice issued guidelines and procedures required by the Cybersecurity Act of 2015. These guidelines provide both the Federal Government and the private sector with an understanding of how to share cyber threat indicators with the DHS National Cybersecurity and Communications Integration Center (NCCIC).

DHS and DOJ issued a separate guidance for the private sector. Today, I would like to hear from our witnesses, their take on the DHS and DOJ private-sector guidance. Now that this committee has written and passed useful legislation giving the DHS authorities to use and share its threat intelligence with private companies, and for companies to do the same with Government in return, and DHS has published guidelines, it is our responsibility in Congress to oversee the realization of a mature risk management process for information security, and I hope we will hear some of the risk-based management approaches today.

Given the complexity of emerging threat capabilities, the link between physical and cyber domains and the diversity of cyber criminals, I would like to hear what challenges the private sector faces in working with the Department of Homeland Security.

For Congress to continue to make effective cybersecurity policy, whether it is related to cyber hygiene or infrastructure protection, it is our job to understand not only the scope of the problem, but also how our public and private sectors work together to enhance security.

Mr. Chairman, as an aside, for the past few weeks, cyber space headlines have been littered with high-profile cases. From the as-yet-to-be determined cyber-based electric grid problems in Ukraine, to a California hospital ransom-ware event . . . in which the hospital did not tell anyone about until after they had paid the ransom . . . to the encryption dilemma surrounding law enforcement access to some of the data on the mobile phone of a home-grown terrorist.

All of which need careful consideration, investigation, and deliberation. I would suggest that to make progress on all of these issues, we need to tone down the confrontational speech-making, rather than remaining on this argumentative, and adversarial highway.

————

STATEMENT OF TOM PATTERSON, VP/GM SECURITY, UNISYS CORPORATION

FEBRUARY 25, 2016

EMERGING CYBER THREATS TO THE UNITED STATES

Unisys appreciates the opportunity to contribute to the Congressional efforts to mitigate cyber threats to the United States, and share our new and advanced concept that we are using to protect both governments and businesses around the world. Cyber attacks are increasing, and leaders in Government and industry are seeking new approaches to protect critical data.

We all rely on computing and communications systems that are critical to financial markets, health care providers, energy producers, schools, governments, and business enterprises. It is not just our computers that are at risk. Increasingly, cyber attacks jeopardize careers, wallets, companies, infrastructure, and even lives. Adversaries boldly wield the power to access personal and corporate data on-line and take control of systems throughout our interconnected world. Recently, we have watched as companies, governments, and institutions report system breaches on a nearly weekly basis. It is clear that core assumptions and approaches that defined old security models are failing.

Unisys provides hundreds of organizations with support for their security requirements for hundreds of organizations. Our clients understand that the original approaches to cybersecurity are no longer working.

Unisys is delivering a fresh approach to security to our clients. The new approach accounts for modem infrastructure—employees that work from home, users that need access to information on mobile devices, data that uses the efficiencies of the cloud, and supply chains that are integrated and interdependent. The new approach also adapts to changes in the adversaries, who are becoming more skilled and more motivated.

Furthermore, we understand that new cybersecurity systems need to assume that infiltrations will somehow occur and must provide tools to localize, limit, and contain the damage.

At the core of our new approach is the advanced concept of micro-segmentation. If segmentation is analogous to a bank vault, micro-segmentation is akin to the many safe deposit boxes within the vault. Micro-segmentation is much more secure and inclusive, and easier to implement and manage. It embraces new technologies like clouds, and new business models like integrated supply chains, while still supporting all the older existing investments. It delivers real results that are both cost-effective and resource-efficient. In order to deliver on the promise of advanced micro-segmentation, Unisys has developed an award winning product—Stealth™— that makes it fast and easy to protect enterprises around the world more securely.

Micro-segmentation allows enterprise managers to divide physical networks quickly and easily into hundreds or thousands of logical micro-networks, or micro-segments. Setting up micro-segments keeps the different parts of an organization logically separate, thus lowering the intrusion risk. If a breach happens, the intruder can only see one segment.

Micro-segmentation works at the internet packet level, cryptographically sealing each packet so that only packets within the approved micro-segment are processed. For every packet, the data is completely encrypted, and the routing information in the headers is cryptographically sealed to ensure only authorized delivery. Users can only send and receive packets for a specified group.

Micro-segmentation is implemented by software, and it therefore operates independently from any given network topology or network hardware. Organizations have a single security model that works equally well in data centers and the public cloud. With micro-segmentation, organizations can extend security to the cloud while retaining control of data in motion and the keys that secure it. Micro-segmentation enables access to the benefits of the cloud—cost savings and network flexibility—without sacrificing security. Micro-segmentation can also be implemented quickly and easily within virtual machines to defend against side-channel attacks and other risks that are specific to cloud architectures.

Micro-segmentation makes it easier to integrate component suppliers by providing just the right amount of access. Micro-segmentation can also protect legacy systems, allowing organizations to use older operating systems while keeping them isolated from newer systems. By embracing a new approach to cybersecurity, we can dramatically increase the strength of our networks and confront the new threat with new tools.

The benefits to adding micro-segmentation to existing networks—in data centers, devices, clouds, and even industrial control systems—are many. It lower costs, affords better protection, and changes catastrophes into small manageable events. It works on outdated systems as well as the most advanced industrial control system, and it does not require expensive hardware or armies of security experts to install or operate it.

Unisys is proud to be a leading provider of advanced micro-segmentation products and services to governments and the private sector. White papers, use cases, demos, and greater technical detail are available on *www.unisys.com/stealth*. Thank for you the opportunity to provide Unisys's perspective on cybersecurity.

––––––––

LETTER FROM THE SOCIETY FOR MAINTENANCE & RELIABILITY PROFESSIONALS

FEBRUARY 24, 2016.

The Honorable JOHN RATCLIFFE,
Chairman, U.S. House Subcommittee on Cybersecurity, Infrastructure Protection, and Security Technologies, 176 Ford House Office Building, Washington, DC 20515.

The Honorable CEDRIC RICHMOND,
Ranking Member, U.S. House Subcommittee on Cybersecurity, Infrastructure Protection, and Security Technologies, 117 Ford House Office Building, Washington, DC 20515.

Subject: SMRP Comments on Emerging Cyber Threats to the United States

DEAR CHAIRMAN RATCLIFFE AND RANKING MEMBER RICHMOND: I am writing to provide comments on emerging cyber threats to the United States. The Society for Maintenance & Reliability Professionals (SMRP) applauds the U.S. House Committee on Homeland Security's decision to hold a congressional hearing within its Subcommittee on Cybersecurity, Infrastructure Protection, and Security Technologies. The maintenance and reliability of cybersecurity systems and critical infrastructure is essential to the security of our nation. Please accept these comments as part of the official record of the subcommittee hearing.

I. SMRP INTRODUCTION AND BACKGROUND

SMRP is a professional society formed in 1992 to develop and promote excellence in the maintenance, reliability, and physical asset management profession. SMRP members consist of engineers, operations managers, repair and reliability technicians, worksite and project planners, and other service providers. SMRP members are experts in specification, design, purchasing, installation, inspection, testing, maintaining, decommissioning, and asset disposal.

Maintenance and reliability jobs are skilled positions that provide competitive advantages to the companies that have them. Companies with highly trained, certified engineers reap a variety of benefits, including lower operations and manufacturing costs, reduced onsite injury risks, reduced environmental risks, and increased net profits. Nearly every industry sector requires the services of maintenance, reliability, and physical asset management personnel, including energy, oil and gas, pharmaceuticals, automotive, government and military, petrochemical, education, and commercial. Our ranks are made up of senior reliability managers from such companies as Cargill, BP, General Electric, General Motors, as well as utilities, Government facilities, and the organizations that support them.

II. MAINTENANCE & RELIABILITY CERTIFICATIONS

Certified Maintenance & Reliability Professional

With over 4,800 accredited professionals certified by SMRP, the Certified Maintenance & Reliability Professional program is the leading credentialing program for verifying the knowledge, skills, and abilities of maintenance and reliability professionals, regardless of education background or work experience. Examining more than just textbook information, the Certified Maintenance & Reliability Professional examination is a thorough assessment of a broader scope of expertise measured against a universal standard. A foundational belief in developing this examination is that professionals in the maintenance and reliability profession learn critical knowledge, skills, and abilities from a variety of sources, both on the job and from outside training.

The Certified Maintenance & Reliability Professional is accredited by the American National Standards Institute (ANSI), which follows International Organization for Standardization (ISO) standards for its accreditation and processes. It was developed to assess professionals' aptitude within the 5 pillars of the Maintenance and Reliability Body of Knowledge: Business management, equipment reliability, manufacturing process reliability, organization and leadership, and work management.

Certified Maintenance & Reliability Technician

The Certified Maintenance & Reliability Technician program is the leading credentialing program for the knowledge, skills, and abilities of maintenance and reliability technicians, regardless of education background or work experience. Earning the Certified Maintenance & Reliability Technician credential indicates that you have achieved a level of ability consistent with the requirements for competence on the job as a multi-skilled maintenance and reliability technician, recognized across all industries in the manufacturing world. A foundational belief in developing this examination is that technicians in the maintenance and reliability profession learn critical knowledge, skills, and abilities from a variety of sources, both on the job and from outside training.

The certification assesses the knowledge and skills of those responsible for preventative, predictive, and corrective maintenance, who are multi-skilled individuals with a critical role in the success of organizations world-wide. The Certified Maintenance & Reliability Technician exam tests competency and knowledge of specific tasks within 4 domains: Maintenance practices, preventative and predictive maintenance, troubleshooting and analysis, and corrective maintenance.

III. CYBER ATTACK AT TARGET STORES

On November 15, 2013, a complex cyber-attack was conducted on Target stores through credentials obtained from a third-party HVAC service company. Once cyber-criminals acquired access to a beachhead in their contractor billing, contract submission, and project management system, they were able to use information provided via the portal to access Target's credit card terminals. Over the next month, the cyber-criminals were able to access over 110 million consumer credit cards.

IV. SMRP CYBERSECURITY POSITIONS AND RECOMMENDATIONS

While a focus on the larger organizations is important for a last line of defense, preventing cyber-attacks on small and medium organizations that service the larger organizations and critical infrastructure should be a primary line of defense. It is SMRP's belief that an understanding of the threats through contractors and subcontractors, regardless of size, and the development of cyber-defense processes will further reduce the risk to the economy and infrastructure of the United States and our allies.

SMRP recommends research into the potential threat through the first line of defense and the inter-connectivity between companies, vendors, contractors, and subcontractors with a goal to establish a cyber-defense strategy. This includes the evaluation of cyber-information and cyber-physical systems as weil as best methods to prevent infiltration and damage to the front-line organizations. This will have the additional impact of improving the security of small business while reducing the number of attacks on larger organizations as current business models by all organizations includes contracting services.

V. SUMMARY AND RECOMMENDATIONS

The maintenance and reliability of cybersecurity systems and critical infrastructure is essential to the security of our nation. We need to better understand the threats posed through contractors and subcontractors in order to truly reduce the risk to the economy and infrastructure. SMRP recommends research into the potential threat through the first line of defense and the inter-connectivity between companies, vendors, contractors, and subcontractors with a goal to establish a cyber-defense strategy.

Thank you for your consideration and please do not hesitate to contact me if you have any questions.

Sincerely,

JOHN FERRARO,
SMRP Government Relations Director.

Mr. RATCLIFFE. The Chair now recognizes the gentlelady from Texas, Ms. Jackson Lee, for 5 minutes of questions.

Ms. JACKSON LEE. I thank the Chair very much.

To the Ranking Member of the subcommittee and, of course, the full committee Chairs and Ranking Member, let me speak quickly. Some bells have started to ring. I want to just join and say I think our committee made a very important step when we passed the Cybersecurity Information-Sharing Act of 2015, and I take note of the bipartisan work on this committee on these issues, even though I think more than a decade ago we began to see the unraveling of the issue of cybersecurity and the sort of importance of going head on in the private sector with 80-plus percent of the cyber world versus the Federal Government.

I think all of us were lagging in the response. So even though we have made some steps in the Judiciary Committee—for example, today, we were discussing the interests of international law enforcement, trying to store data in many of our providers. So everywhere there are questions of either breaching, because someone wants the information, or breaching when someone should not be getting the information.

Let me cite a very quick example on this issue of ransomware. The latest victim, Hollywood Presbyterian, 9,420 beds, and which was forced to pay 4 bitcoins on-line, $17,000, to get access to their own patient and administrative computer networks.

Police departments have fallen victim. So let me ask the question, does anywhere know how often ransomware is used to get ransom from victims? Are there requirements to report ransomware attacks or should there be? Anyone care to comment on that?

Ms. KOLDE. We are seeing an increase in the use of ransomware, and where initially it seemed to be a fairly background noise-level type of attack used by amateur criminals largely against individuals, we are now seeing it being used against corporations, both in terms of the ransomware itself where the data is encrypted and in terms of other types of extortion. Basically, the criminals are becoming emboldened.

If you are an organization, particularly one that may provide criminal services or support critical infrastructure, you can't afford to not be operational, whether that is due to ransomware or due to the fact that someone is threatening to wipe data on your computer and destroy your assets.

So I think that that trend is going to continue. I am not aware of any current reporting requirements outside of the current regulatory framework, but I don't think that those attacks are going to slow down anytime soon.

Ms. JACKSON LEE. Would it be helpful—first of all, you know, fact finding and facts are probably part of a cure, may not be the total cure. I think it would be helpful for us to be aware, policymakers, about these attacks. Would you welcome that, at least providing us with that—when I say providing, through the regulatory scheme?

Ms. KOLDE. I would prefer to consider the business impact of that, as well. But I think that again generalizing the more we know about what is going on, the more we are aware of what specific things we need to defend against, and how we need to promote education around those issues.

Ms. JACKSON LEE. Maybe anyone else, but, Mr. Bromwich, does Symantec recommend or use backdoors in their cybersecurity products?

Mr. BROMWICH. We most definitely do not. We most definitely do not recommend the use of backdoors in really any situation. Backdoors compromise security technologies. Backdoors compromise the integrity of encryption technologies. We strongly believe that those should not be compromised.

Ms. JACKSON LEE. As I ask this question, I want you to think of multifactor identification, meaning two methods are used to be sure the person giving computer access or who they claim they are, that sort of goes the overall question of the ransomware and others.

But let me ask this question that I hope that I can get any of you to jump in. The United States critical infrastructure is already dependent on our Nation's cyber networks and systems. These sectors are also increasingly interdependent, and the disruption is obviously massive. What are some of the unique cybersecurity challenges critical infrastructure—and that is across the gamut, the electric grid, et cetera, that I have been looking at—owners and operators face? Are there any particularly emerging cyber threats that are unique to the critical infrastructure?

I have some articles that I want to submit into the record on the port, but can any of you jump in on any of those that you see?

Ms. KOLDE. I think one of the things to keep in mind about critical infrastructure is there has been a lot of concern, and very relevant concern, about critical infrastructure being subjected highly-sophisticated targeted attacks, and that is definitely a concern. Those attacks will primarily come from very well-resourced threat actors, most likely nation-states.

But I think it is important to keep in mind that critical infrastructure can be impacted by other types of attacks, as well. There may be threat groups that are interested in doing something opportunistic, where they don't care specifically if it is a port, a specific dam, a particular power plant that is affected, but they want to make a very public statement that they can do this sort of thing.

So any particular part of critical infrastructure that may happen to be vulnerable may be a target to simply something like a destructive attack. Like any other organization, those types of critical infrastructure organizations are also potentially subject to damaging attacks that are simply incidental, the wrong virus, the wrong piece of malware that gets into the network and shuts down computers, without necessarily impacting control systems or infrastructure itself, could still put that utility, that financial system out of business until they recover.

So it is important to keep aware of the whole spectrum of threats that are potentially impacting those organizations.

Ms. JACKSON LEE. Mr. Chairman, may I submit—I saw Dr. Porche, but maybe you can answer in writing—it looked like you were on the verge—but in any event, let me ask unanimous consent to put into the record "Nine Major Models of Internet-Connected Baby Monitors are Extremely Vulnerable to Hacking." As I looked at Mr. Richmond, he may have an interest in this. I know I have 2 twin 8-month-olds, and they are, as they say, using new technology.

So I ask unanimous consent to submit that into the record. It makes this hearing very important, Mr. Chairman.

Mr. RATCLIFFE. Without objection.

[The information follows:]

ARTICLE SUBMITTED BY HONORABLE SHEILA JACKSON LEE

NINE MAJOR MODELS OF INTERNET-CONNECTED BABY MONITORS ARE EXTREMELY VULNERABLE TO HACKING

SECURITY RESEARCHERS COULD HACK INTO HOME-MONITORING SYSTEMS WITH EASE

http://www.consumeraffairs.com/news/nine-major-models-of-internet-connected-baby-monitors-are-extremely-vulnerable-to-hacking-090315.html

09/03/2015, ConsumerAffairs, By Jennifer Abel

Ever since wireless or Internet-connected home baby monitors and security systems became commonplace, there have been equally commonplace warnings about how easily hackers can break into these systems.

There even exist voyeurism websites dedicated to streaming or archiving camera footage from unprotected Internet protocol (IP) cameras—almost always without the camera owners' knowledge. Last April, for example, a Minnesota family learned this the hard way after they discovered that hackers had hijacked the "nanny cam" in their baby's room—and posted surreptitious baby photos on a foreign website.

Yet recent research by the Rapid7 cybersecurity firm suggests that the majority of home baby monitors on the market today remain extremely vulnerable to hack attacks. Rapid7's white-hat hackers were successfully able to exploit vulnerabilities in 9 different models of baby monitor. Worse yet, many of those vulnerabilities are inherent to their systems—meaning that even security-conscious and tech-savvy users cannot fix them. Mark Stanislav and Tod Beardsley co-wrote Rapid7's report, which is available as a .pdf here.

Increased hacking threat

Most baby-monitor-hacking stories emphasize the obvious privacy threats to the baby and others in the house. But Stanislav and Beardsley, in their executive summary, pointed out that the threat stretches much farther than that:

While Rapid7 is not aware of specific campaigns of mass exploitation of consumer-grade IoT [Internet of things] devices, this paper should serve as an advisory on the growing risk that businesses face as their employees accumulate more of these interconnected devices on their home networks.

This is especially relevant today, as employees increasingly blur the lines between home networks and business networks through routine telecommuting and data storage on cloud resources shared between both contexts.

In other words: any Internet connection, or device with one, has the potential to be hacked. And if a hacker successfully breaches security for one of your Internet-connected devices, there's a good chance he can piggyback from there to breach the security of anything else connected to it.

So let's say a hacker secretly breaches your baby-cam or other home-security network. You then use your smartphone to watch camera footage while you're out running errands; now the hacker can get into your smartphone. And when you use the phone to check your messages at work, that gives the hackers access to your corporate network, so your personal, private hacking problem might now place the entire company you work for at risk.

Though the risk to your family is bad enough. Just last week, an unknown hacker used a breached baby monitor to harass a family in Indianapolis.

Jared Denman said that his wife was playing with their 2-year-old daughter when the baby monitor suddenly started playing music: the 1980s creepy-stalker anthem "Every Breath You Take," by The Police. Once the hacker realized he had the mother's attention, he started making "sexual noises" over the speaker. Turns out the Denmans, like many baby-monitor buyers, had made the mistake of not changing the system's factory-set username and passwords, which meant anyone who knew them could break in.

Monitoring devices fail security test

Yet even consumers savvy enough to avoid such obvious mistakes still can't be certain their privacy is protected when there's a baby monitor in the house. When Rapid7 tested 9 different models of baby monitors, said Mark Stanislav, "Eight of the 9 cameras got an F and one got a D minus.

"Every camera had one hidden account that a consumer can't change because it's hard coded or not easily accessible. Whether intended for admin or support, it gives an outsider backdoor access to the camera."

The tested baby monitors included various models produced by Gyonii, Philips, Lens Peek-a-view, Summer Baby Zoom, TRENDnet, WiFiBaby, Withing, and iBaby. A chart on page 7 of Rapidis report (page 9 of the online .pdf) lists the vulnerabilities found in each specific model.

Some security flaws were more glaring than others. The Philips In.Sight model, according to Stanislav, streams live video onto the Internet without so much as requiring a password or account to protect it. With Summer Baby Zoom, the researchers learned, there's no authentication process to allow new viewers to see specific camera feeds; anyone who wishes to can simply add themselves.

According to the timelines in Rapidis report, the researchers informed various vendors of these security flaws in early July. Yet Stanislav said that of all the companies he contacted, Philips was the only responsive vendor.

Protect your privacy

While the vulnerabilities exposed by Rapid7 can't be entirely eradicated, there are ways users can reduce the possibility of electronic eavesdropping. For example, unencrypted video files or other data is most vulnerable to hacking when viewed over a public WiFi network, so if you must remotely view unencrypted video, Stanislav recommends using a cell phone Internet connection instead.

Parents should also keep baby monitors unplugged when they're not in use, use secure passwords, change them frequently, and make sure the device's software is always up-to-date. You might also consider setting up a search-engine email alert so that you are notified anytime a news story mentioning your model of baby monitor gets published; if new security flaws or fixes are announced, that would probably be the quickest, easiest way to ensure you hear about it.

Ms. JACKSON LEE. Then finally, what if cybersecurity—this article, I am sorry, *Consumer Affairs* dated 9/3/2015—and then "What If A Cybersecurity Attack Shut Down Our Ports?", October 7, 2015, and this is not stopping cargo ships, but actually causing the loss of knowing where products are, like clothes, electronics, food, and everything. I ask unanimous consent to put that into the record. Thank you.

Mr. RATCLIFFE. Without objection.

[The information follows:]

ARTICLE SUBMITTED BY HONORABLE SHEILA JACKSON LEE

WHAT IF A CYBERSECURITY ATTACK SHUT DOWN OUR PORTS?

IT'S A REAL, AND FRIGHTENING, POSSIBILITY

SLATE MAGAZINE, October 7, 2015, by Lily Hay Newman

*http://www.slate.com/articles/technology/future_tense/2015/05/
maritime_cybersecurity_ports_are_unsecured.html*

Shipping containers lie stacked upon a yard at Port Newark Container Terminal, the third-largest cargo terminal in New York harbor on February 21, 2006 in Newark, New Jersey.

The real Internet of Things: Shipping containers lie stacked upon a yard at Port Newark Container Terminal, the third-largest cargo terminal in New York harbor, on Feb. 21, 2006 in Newark, New Jersey.

It's easy to forget when you're on dry land that 90 percent of the world's goods are shipped on boats. While we worry about the cybersecurity of power grids and nuclear missile silos, most of us have never thought about whether the container ships and ports that bring us our clothes, electronics, food—everything—are secured against digital threats.

The April newsletter from maritime cybersecurity consulting firm CyberKeel contained a scary stat. According to a spot check the group conducted, 37 percent of maritime companies with Windows webservers haven't been keeping up with installing security patches from Microsoft. As a result, more than one-third of these sites are vulnerable to denial-of-service attacks and certain types of remote access.

We already know that companies are slow to protect their networks. On the first anniversary of the discovery of Heartbleed last month, one study showed that 74 percent of companies on the Forbes Global 2000 list hadn't comprehensively patched their systems against what was possibly the worst vulnerability ever discovered. Maritime companies, though, are responsible not just for customer data (which is already extremely valuable), but for physical goods. If their systems suffer an outage, companies might not know where their ships are, or ports might not be able to unload cargo. Doesn't this sound kind of, um, important?

Over the last few years, groups around the world have been working to bring maritime cybersecurity to the fore and begin talking about the reality of the threats. When breaches occur, private companies currently have virtually no incentive to disclose them, because it will only generate bad publicity and breed distrust among customers and investors. Incidents have started to come out, and this first step toward transparency is promising.

But those steps are taking a little too long, given how critical maritime infrastructure is to everyday functioning in the U.S. and abroad. A 2013 report on maritime cybersecurity from Brookings explained, "The potential consequences of even a minimal disruption of the flow of goods in U.S. ports would be high . . . [S]helves at grocery stores and gas tanks at service stations would run empty."

When 90 percent of goods come through maritime shipping, it's not that hard to imagine that situation coming to fruition. CyberKeel co-founder Lars Jensen says that when he and partner Morten Schenk began working on maritime cybersecurity consulting in January 2014, the prevailing idea among maritime executives was that digital threats either didn't exist or were highly theoretical. But, he says, "The thing that started to scare us a little bit was that some of things . . . where we said, 'This is clearly Hollywood-scenario stuff' had already happened."

Many of the incidents that have occurred have, as you might expect, been kept quiet. But examples are trickling out. For example, at a January public meeting to discuss maritime cybersecurity standards, the Coast Guard said that in 2014, a U.S. port (it's not clear which one) suffered a 7-hour GPS signal disruption that crippled operations. Port cranes use GPS data to establish their own positions, the positions of the containers they are supposed to move, and the positions to where they are supposed to move the containers. The incident the Coast Guard described affected 4 cranes. Without GPS, ports have to switch to manual operation, which is extremely inefficient and time-consuming.

Four confused cranes probably don't quite evoke the mayhem that the phrase Hollywood-scenario stuff might conjure in your mind. But remember that GPS is also crucial for navigation on board ships and for tracking the whereabouts of different vessels as they move. Jensen describes one possible scenario (which he says he hasn't heard about actually happening yet) in which hackers could use GPS jamming as a way of holding a ship hostage, asking a small enough ransom that it's cheaper for the shipping company to just pay rather than attempt to intervene.

GPS's ubiquity is both its strength and weakness. "The government provides positioning, navigation, and timing through the GPS system," says Dana Goward, president of the Resilient Navigation and Timing Foundation and the former maritime navigation authority for the United States. "It's a free, highly precise signal that engineers have incorporated into virtually every technology. But because of that, it's become a single point of failure for much of America. And you see examples of that in maritime." The RNT Foundation advocates for the creation of a GPS alternative for emergencies. A 2004 Presidential security directive to the Department of Transportation supported the initiative, but 11 years later, it still hasn't moved forward.

Another troubling incident occurred in 2012, when malware took out about three-quarters of Saudi Aramco's files across tens of thousands of PCs. An image of a burning American flag appeared on every screen. The company was able to contain and mitigate the attack relatively quickly, but since the oil company distributes its product through maritime shipping, it was a wakeup call about how big of an economic impact a port-related hack could have.

In March, Rutgers University held a maritime cybersecurity conference co-sponsored by the Command, Control, and Interoperability Center for Advanced Data Analysis and the American Military University. "The threat is very real," said Rear Adm. Marshall Lytle, the assistant commandant responsible for U.S. Coast Guard Cyber Command and the keynote speaker at the conference. "These intrusions and attacks are taking place every minute and every second of every day."

One of the problems with incentivizing both disclosures and increased cybersecurity vigilance is the lack of international or even domestic port standards from governing bodies. "Right now there is nothing akin to the [International Ship and Port Facility Security Code] rules on the cyber side. Nothing whatsoever," Jensen said. (The ISPS Code is a set of internationally agreed-upon minimum standards for physical ship and port security that was developed after 9/11 and enacted in 2004.) "There has to be some sort of consensus coalescing in the industry."

At the Rutgers conference, Vice Adm. Charles Michel, who is deputy commandant for operations, outlined some of the Coast Guard's plans for cybersecurity strategy. "Probably the most important part of the Coast Guard's Cyber Strategy is in its key organizing principle: The strategy is all about embracing a policy framework that will allow our enterprise to begin to tackle these challenges."

The issue hasn't exactly reached peak urgency in either the private or government sector, but Goward thinks it needs to. "The sooner the better," he says. "Opportunities for mistakes or for bad people to do malicious things just continue to grow. The solution can't come soon enough."

This article is part of Future Tense, a collaboration among Arizona State University, New America, and Slate. Future Tense explores the ways emerging technologies affect society, policy, and culture. To read more, visit the Future Tense blog and the Future Tense home page. You can also follow us on Twitter.

Ms. JACKSON LEE. I yield back.

Mr. RATCLIFFE. I thank the gentlelady. The Chair now recognizes the gentleman from New York, Mr. Donovan.

Mr. DONOVAN. Thank you, Mr. Chairman. The next set of bells you are going to see all of us run, so let me speak quickly.

This Congress passed a remarkable piece of legislation recently in cybersecurity and sharing of information. What should we be looking to do now in the current year, in 2016? Is there anything in particular that we should be doing now? I mean, the sharing of information was an issue. We kind of resolved part of that. What should we be looking at now as a legislative body to help you? Anyone?

Mr. PORCHE. I will chime in first.

Mr. DONOVAN. Thank you, Doctor.

Mr. PORCHE. So, one—you may not like this answer, sir—but a little bit of wait. Let's see how well CISA works. You know, if the protections in place are valid, if the voluntary nature of the bill is still successful, people are chiming in. So let's see how successful that is, and if there need to be any changes.

Maybe far into the future, when we can sort-of work out the privacy and the civil liberties issues that will likely come up, start thinking about, how do we take advantage of this information? How do we fuse all the different sources and all the contextual information that Ms. Kolde talked about to give us a better picture?

So we have kind of—the CISA 2015 bill got us into the information age, despite the fact we have been in the information age for a while. What is next is the knowledge age, where we can actually pull smarts, pull intelligent fusion, pull sense-making out of all that data that we have coming in, doing something quite useful with the data that is collected that can give us insights into the next attack.

That is in the future, but we should be thinking about, you know, discussing how do we get there?

Mr. CILLUFFO. Mr. Donovan, a couple of quick thoughts. One—and I touched on in my prepared remarks and maybe in the oral—to examine the active defense set of issues, in terms of—there is a lot of policy space behind build higher walls and bigger moats and hack back. Between that space, we have got to start identifying what some of the actions and steps companies can take to more proactively defend their systems. They can't afford to wait. If Government is not going to respond, someone needs to be able to respond.

So looking at what those particular rules of the road are, taking a close examination of the CFAA, the Computer Fraud and Abuse Act, I think needs to be part of that.

Then the bigger thing—and this may be more of a political question—but the reality is, is we have got to articulate a deterrence strategy. Right now, our adversaries are operating with impunity. Until we can raise the bar, raise the cost for their behavior, induce changes in that behavior, we are going to be playing defense the whole time. You know what? I don't care what—and we have got the best companies in the world here—but we are never going to be able to firewall our way out of this problem.

We are going to have to be able to lean forward, and that is going to include some policy decisions and integrate that into our overall National security planning process.

Ms. KOLDE. From a practice standpoint, again, looking specifically to things that we can do to better defend and educate, I think the information exchange is a really good step forward. I think we should start looking ahead not only to see how that is going to play out in practice, but what can we do to exchange richer types of information, not just context around the indicators themselves, but countermeasures and recommendations for how to respond.

In addition, continuing to look for creative defensive measures, technological as well as best practices from individuals that we can continue to promulgate out in the private and public sector for how networks can better defend themselves.

Mr. BROMWICH. I would also jump on that and say that an additional—there is more work to be done on the sharing front. I think we are doing a good job increasing the sharing that is happening in industry. We would like it to be more of a two-way street with Government. That would definitely be much more helpful.

Then finally, just more—you know, a lot more education and emphasis on the technologies that are out there that are available, to encourage their adoption, to build awareness. There still just is not nearly enough awareness of the technologies that are available and how important the problem is.

Mr. DONOVAN. Many of you hit on this, and the Chairman and many of my colleagues spoke about anticipation of the new type of attacks. I kind of equate this—because I am a layman—that is this like a disease, we wait for the disease to happen, and then we find a cure? Do we wait for attacks—because I suspect there are different ways that people attack our systems—and then try to figure out how to deal with it? Or do we anticipate what is the next method of attack and try to protect ourselves from that before it happens?

Mr. BROMWICH. We definitely anticipate. I mean, everything that we do is entirely focused on being proactive and ahead of the threat. Unfortunately for many individuals and enterprises and government, it tends to be very reactive. They don't put the protection in place until they are hit.

Those protections are there. They are designed to be proactive. We are constantly watching what is happening in the threat landscape to understand where we need to go with the technology so that we can get ahead of the attacker.

Ms. KOLDE. I think a lot of the good anticipation comes out of the security research community itself. In my career in IT, everything is theoretical until it is not. So if you see some of the briefings coming out of the private sector or the commercial world at conferences like Black Hat, people who are researching interesting new techniques, new ways to exploit devices, new vulnerabilities that may show up on the horizon, those start out as research and they become reality.

During the past year, we have seen an increasing number of attacks against network infrastructure devices, people going after routers. Those types of attacks were discussed at Black Hat as far back as 2007 as part of the research community where we are now seeing them in the wild.

Mr. DONOVAN. Thank you all. I yield back, Mr. Chairman.

Mr. RATCLIFFE. I thank the gentleman. I now recognize myself for 5 minutes.

I want to focus on some nation-state concerns, and I am going to start with you, Ms. Kolde, because some of the trends and developments have started in Russia, and you have talked about that in your testimony a little bit. So I really have a two-part question.

First part is: Is it concerning to you that Russia and/or Russian actors seem less concerned about being attributed? Then the second part of my question is: Based on James Clapper's testimony and the establishment of a Russian cyber command, what do you think the implications are of this? Is it a game-changer for Russia? What is FireEye seeing in terms of threat reporting in connection with that, if anything?

Ms. KOLDE. I can speak most directly to the first part of your question in terms of what we are actually seeing. Historically, Russia has operated in a very stealthy manner. They were always assumed to be very skilled at what they did, but we typically did not see them operating.

What has changed over the past few years is that we have had more visibility into their activity, there has been much more public reporting of what they are doing, and despite that public reporting, we do not see them changing their tactics. So they are being talked about in the press and the media and the security community, and they are continuing to operate.

We have also gotten to see some actors that we suspect very strongly are Russian nation-state through some of our incident response engagements. They have been extremely aggressive within victim environments. Some threat groups when they are detected will go silent and they will abandon the network, so that they just disappear once you know that they are there.

We have had engagements where we have been working with Russian threat groups where they fight very strongly to stay within that network, and they do so with a great deal of skill and adaptability that challenged even our responders to keep ahead of them.

So they are very determined and they are very well-resourced. Again, I don't see that changing operationally, unless something specific would cause them to do that.

In terms of Russia establishing a cyber command, that speaks more to policy, which is not my strong suit, but I think it just shows that nation-states in general are going to continue to see the cyber realm as a realm of engagement, similar to any other military, economic, political forum, and that is going to continue.

They have clearly stated their intent to keep playing in that world, and they have the skill and resources to be a very powerful player.

Mr. RATCLIFFE. Let me—thank you. Let me shift to Iran and something, Mr. Cilluffo, based on your research, as we all know, the administration announced a nuclear agreement with Iran and lifted a number of sanctions.

Can you give me your thoughts on whether or not Iran may move beyond the denial-of-service attacks into more destructive malware attacks against our critical infrastructure as a result of that Iranian nuclear deal that I referenced in my opening and influx of cash?

Mr. CILLUFFO. Well, Mr. Chairman, that is the $64,000 question, because I do think there are some legitimate concerns and considerations in terms of not only do they have additional cash to be able to devote to building out their computer network attack capabilities, but they had shown that they were willing to turn to those tools for quite some time now.

Historically, Iran was home to one of the most sophisticated hacking underground communities. The Ashiyane network, and many others have been in business for an awful long time. During the so-called green revolution, the way they were able to turn to basically shut down access to anyone inside Iran to the rest of the world was a clear indicator that they have some of those capabilities.

I think most importantly, though, is that they are willing to work with proxies. Clearly, when you look at the energy sector in particular, this is an area I think we need to be very concerned about.

Let me just underscore one point, because—and it gets to the question on Russia, as well—when we think of cyber, we can't treat it in isolation of the overall strategies and objectives that these nations may have. So the Russian computer network attack and Cyber Command capability is an extension of what they have been engaging militarily, diplomatically, and through other means for quite some time. To them, it is about psychological operation. It is perception management, first and foremost. It is computer network attack second.

Same goes with Iran. The big question is, is whether or not cyber is off the table. Is it off the table? I think we need to make explicitly clear that it better be.

Mr. RATCLIFFE. My last question—thank you—my last question—and I am going to try and give all of you a chance to answer it—relates to something I said in my opening about the fact that despite the increasing magnitude and number of cyber attacks that we are seeing, we are seeing in my opinion little response or a clear deterrent strategy from this administration.

Now, if you agree with that opinion—you may or may not—but if you do, what actions should the United States take, in your opinion, to clearly articulate that there are serious consequences for those types of actions?

I will go down the row. Start with you, Mr. Cilluffo.

Mr. CILLUFFO. I have been pretty vocal on this, so I do feel that we have not articulated and certainly haven't demonstrated a cyber deterrence strategy. While I think there has been recognition that we need to be moving in that direction—and I think Secretary Carter, Ash Carter at the Department of Defense has glommed onto this issue as a priority, I think is important. But what is the litmus test?

Is OPM, the OPM hack, would that have been a litmus test to be able to demonstrate a commensurate sort of response? I think we have had enough of those litmus tests. So the question is, is, if we articulate it, we better be willing to signal and respond. So assuming that we do get our arms around this, we better have the political wherewithal then to be able to respond, and not only through cyber means.

At the end of the day, cyber is its own domain, but it transcends air, land, sea, space. So the question is, is: Where do we have the greatest strength? When are we willing to utilize these tools?

Mr. RATCLIFFE. I realize, Ms. Kolde and Mr. Bromwich, you may or may not want to weigh in on that question, but feel free to.

Ms. KOLDE. Yes, I think the one step that is needed is obviously a clear articulation of our policy. I won't personally speak to what that policy should or should not be, but we need to be clear about what that policy is and what we may or may not do in response.

One thing I would like to point out with respect to that is regardless of the consequences, if we are going to implement some form of consequences, we need to be sure we are implementing it against the right nation-state, the right criminal group. The challenge there is in attributing an attack and in being highly confident, fairly quickly, who is actually responsible. That is a big challenge currently.

Mr. CILLUFFO. I agree.

Mr. BROMWICH. Yes, I would agree, the attribution is super difficult. I think the only thing that I would say is that more discussion and more diplomatic outreach so that we can better find and prosecute criminals would be certainly helpful. Today, many of these criminals operate outside of the realm of law.

Mr. RATCLIFFE. Dr. Porche, I will give you the last word.

Mr. PORCHE. Thank you. I would say—and this has been said by panelists here—just remembering that cyber space is one domain. The United States military operates in many other domains. So we have heard press articles talk about potential Iranian hacktivists attacking a U.S. dam. I don't have any information that says it is there. But what prevents nation-states from taking action are the fact that they would have to deal with the United States in other domains.

So it always has to include all domains, not just cyber. Our response to a cyber attack may not be in cyber.

Mr. RATCLIFFE. I thank you all for being here today. Members of the committee may actually have some additional questions for each of you, and I would ask you to respond to those in writing. Pursuant to committee rule 7(e), the hearing record will be open for 10 days. Without objection, the subcommittee stands adjourned. Thank you all.

[Whereupon, at 3:20 p.m., the subcommittee was adjourned.]

○